HUMAN RIGHTS: BACKGROUND AND ISSUES

REFUGEE RESETTLEMENT IN THE UNITED STATES

HUMAN RIGHTS: BACKGROUND AND ISSUES

Additional books in this series can be found on Nova's website under the Series tab.

Additional e-books in this series can be found on Nova's website under the e-book tab.

AMERICA IN THE 21ST CENTURY: POLITICAL AND ECONOMIC ISSUES

Additional books in this series can be found on Nova's website under the Series tab.

Additional e-books in this series can be found on Nova's website under the e-book tab.

HUMAN RIGHTS: BACKGROUND AND ISSUES

REFUGEE RESETTLEMENT IN THE UNITED STATES

RICHARD J. IRVIN
AND
LOIS GAMBRELL
EDITORS

New York

For permission to use material from this book please contact us:
Telephone 631-231-7269; Fax 631-231-8175
Web Site: http://www.novapublishers.com

Additional color graphics may be available in the e-book version of this book.

LIBRARY OF CONGRESS CATALOGING-IN-PUBLICATION DATA

ISBN: 978-1-62257-962-4

Published by Nova Science Publishers, Inc. † New York

CONTENTS

PREFACE

This book provides an overview on the admission of refugees to the United States and their resettlement here which is authorized by the Immigration and Nationality Act (INA), as amended by the Refugee Act of 1980. The 1980 Act had two basic purposes: (1)to provide a uniform procedure for refugee admissions; and (2)to authorize federal assistance to resettle refugees and promote their self-sufficiency. The intent of the legislation was to end an ad hoc approach to refugee admissions and resettlement that had characterized U.S. refugee policy since World War II. Under the INA, a refugee is a person who is outside his or her country and who is unable or unwilling to return because of persecution or a well-founded fear of persecution on account of race, religion, nationality, membership in a particular social group, or political opinion.

Chapter 1 – A refugee is a person fleeing his or her country because of persecution or a well-founded fear of persecution on account of race, religion, nationality, membership in a particular social group, or political opinion. Typically, the annual number of refugees that can be admitted into the United States, known as the refugee ceiling, and the allocation of these numbers by region are set by the President after consultation with Congress at the start of each fiscal year. For FY2012, the worldwide refugee ceiling is 76,000, with 73,000 admissions numbers allocated among the regions of the world and 3,000 numbers comprising an unallocated reserve. An unallocated reserve is to be used if, and where, a need develops for refugee slots in excess of the allocated numbers. The FY2012 regional allocations are, as follows: Africa (12,000), East Asia (18,000), Europe and Central Asia (2,000), Latin America/Caribbean (5,500), and Near East/South Asia (35,500).

Overseas processing of refugees is conducted through a system of three priorities for admission. *Priority 1* comprises cases involving persons facing compelling security concerns. *Priority 2* comprises cases involving persons from specific groups of special humanitarian concern to the United States (e.g., Iranian religious minorities). *Priority 3* comprises family reunification cases involving close relatives of persons admitted as refugees or granted asylum.

Special legislative provisions facilitate relief for certain refugee groups. The "Lautenberg Amendment," which was first enacted in 1989, allows certain former Soviet and Indochinese nationals to qualify for refugee status based on their membership in a protected category with a credible fear of persecution. In 2004, Congress amended the Lautenberg Amendment to add the "Specter Amendment," which requires the designation of categories of Iranian religious minorities whose cases are to be adjudicated under the Lautenberg Amendment's reduced evidentiary standard. Subsequent laws extended the Lautenberg Amendment, as amended by the Specter Amendment, through FY2010. For FY2011, Congress extended the amendment only until June 1, 2011, and it temporarily lapsed on that date. It was re-enacted for FY2012 by P.L. 112-74, however, and is now in effect until October 1, 2012. Another provision, referred to as the "McCain Amendment" or the "McCain-Davis Amendment," had made certain adult children of Vietnamese re-education camp survivors eligible for U.S. refugee resettlement. This amendment was repealed by P.L. 111-117.

The Department of Health and Human Service's Office of Refugee Resettlement (HHS/ORR) administers an initial transitional assistance program for temporarily dependent refugees and Cuban/Haitian entrants.

Chapter 2 – In recent years, the United States has admitted an increasingly diverse group of refugees and other humanitarian cases with a diverse set of needs. There seems to be broad consensus that the U.S. refugee resettlement assistance system is not adequately meeting the needs of these new arrivals and is ripe for reform. The National Security Council is leading an interagency review of refugee resettlement, the forthcoming results of which may further energize reform efforts. To help inform possible future efforts to reform the refugee resettlement assistance system, this report discusses existing resettlement assistance programs, key challenges and issues in providing effective assistance, and policy options to reform the current system.

To assist newly arriving refugees, the Department of State (DOS) administers a program of initial resettlement known as the Reception and Placement Program. Under this program, public and private, nonprofit entities provide new refugees with initial resettlement services and referrals to other services, as needed.

A separate set of refugee resettlement assistance programs, administered by the Office of Refugee Resettlement (ORR) in the Department of Health and Human Services' Administration for Children and Families (HHS/ACF), provides transitional assistance to refugees and other designated groups. These groups include individuals granted asylum, Cuban and Haitian entrants, trafficking victims, Amerasians, and Iraqi and Afghan special immigrants. The ORR programs— which provide mainly cash assistance, medical assistance, and employment-related services—are intended to help the beneficiaries (who are referred to collectively as "refugees" in this report) achieve economic self-sufficiency as soon as possible after their arrival in the United States.

Many observers argue that the DOS and ORR programs and the refugee resettlement assistance system more broadly are in need of reform. A number of reports have identified perceived shortcomings in the existing system and have offered recommendations for change. Several of these reports have focused, in particular, on the recent experience of Iraqi refugees resettled in the United States.

Among the broad challenges facing the refugee resettlement assistance system are interagency coordination and information sharing, and funding. Critics also question the system's self-sufficiency model, which requires refugees to secure employment as quickly as possible. Key issues include financial assistance to refugees, which is widely viewed as insufficient, and the "lottery effect," whereby refugees resettled in different parts of the United States receive different levels of financial assistance and services. Growing out of these challenges and issues are a variety of options for reforming the existing system with respect to administration and planning and the ORR programs.

Chapter 3 – In fiscal year 2011, the United States admitted more than 56,000 refugees under its refugee resettlement program. Upon entry, a network of private, nonprofit voluntary agencies (voluntary agencies) selects the communities where refugees will live. The Department of State's PRM and the Department of Health and Human Services' ORR provide funding to help refugees settle in their communities and obtain employment and monitor implementation of the program.

Congress has begun to reexamine the refugee resettlement program, and GAO was asked to examine (1) the factors resettlement agencies consider when determining where refugees are initially placed; (2) the effects refugees have on their communities; (3) how federal agencies ensure program effectiveness and integrity; and (4) what is known about the integration of refugees. GAO reviewed agency guidance, monitoring protocols, reports, and studies; conducted a literature review; reviewed and analyzed relevant federal and state laws and regulations; and met with federal and state officials, voluntary agency staff, and local stakeholders in eight selected communities.

In: Refugee Resettlement in the United States ISBN: 978-1-62257-962-4
Editors: R. J. Irvin and L. Gambrell

Chapter 1

REFUGEE ADMISSIONS AND RESETTLEMENT POLICY*

Andorra Bruno

SUMMARY

A refugee is a person fleeing his or her country because of persecution or a well-founded fear of persecution on account of race, religion, nationality, membership in a particular social group, or political opinion. Typically, the annual number of refugees that can be admitted into the United States, known as the refugee ceiling, and the allocation of these numbers by region are set by the President after consultation with Congress at the start of each fiscal year. For FY2012, the worldwide refugee ceiling is 76,000, with 73,000 admissions numbers allocated among the regions of the world and 3,000 numbers comprising an unallocated reserve. An unallocated reserve is to be used if, and where, a need develops for refugee slots in excess of the allocated numbers. The FY2012 regional allocations are, as follows: Africa (12,000), East Asia (18,000), Europe and Central Asia (2,000), Latin America/Caribbean (5,500), and Near East/South Asia (35,500).

Overseas processing of refugees is conducted through a system of three priorities for admission. *Priority 1* comprises cases involving persons facing compelling security concerns. *Priority 2* comprises cases involving persons from specific groups of special humanitarian concern

* This is an edited, reformatted and augmented version of Congressional Research Service, Publication No. RL31269, dated March 7, 2012.

to the United States (e.g., Iranian religious minorities). *Priority 3* comprises family reunification cases involving close relatives of persons admitted as refugees or granted asylum.

Special legislative provisions facilitate relief for certain refugee groups. The "Lautenberg Amendment," which was first enacted in 1989, allows certain former Soviet and Indochinese nationals to qualify for refugee status based on their membership in a protected category with a credible fear of persecution. In 2004, Congress amended the Lautenberg Amendment to add the "Specter Amendment," which requires the designation of categories of Iranian religious minorities whose cases are to be adjudicated under the Lautenberg Amendment's reduced evidentiary standard. Subsequent laws extended the Lautenberg Amendment, as amended by the Specter Amendment, through FY2010. For FY2011, Congress extended the amendment only until June 1, 2011, and it temporarily lapsed on that date. It was re-enacted for FY2012 by P.L. 112-74, however, and is now in effect until October 1, 2012. Another provision, referred to as the "McCain Amendment" or the "McCain-Davis Amendment," had made certain adult children of Vietnamese re-education camp survivors eligible for U.S. refugee resettlement. This amendment was repealed by P.L. 111-117.

The Department of Health and Human Service's Office of Refugee Resettlement (HHS/ORR) administers an initial transitional assistance program for temporarily dependent refugees and Cuban/Haitian entrants.

Background and Definitions

The admission of refugees to the United States and their resettlement here are authorized by the Immigration and Nationality Act (INA), as amended by the Refugee Act of 1980.[1]

The 1980 Act had two basic purposes: (1) to provide a uniform procedure for refugee admissions; and (2) to authorize federal assistance to resettle refugees and promote their self-sufficiency. The intent of the legislation was to end an ad hoc approach to refugee admissions and resettlement that had characterized U.S. refugee policy since World War II.

Under the INA, a *refugee* is a person who is outside his or her country and who is unable or unwilling to return because of persecution or a well-founded fear of persecution on account of race, religion, nationality, membership in a particular social group, or political opinion.[2]

In special circumstances, a refugee also may be a person who is within his or her country and who is persecuted or has a well-founded fear of persecution on account of race, religion, nationality, membership in a particular social group, or political opinion. Excluded from the INA definition of a refugee is any person who participated in the persecution of another.[3]

Refugees are processed and admitted to the United States from abroad. The Department of State (DOS) handles overseas processing of refugees and U.S. Citizenship and Immigration Services (USCIS) of the Department of Homeland Security (DHS) makes final determinations about eligibility for admission.

Separate provision is made in the INA for the granting of *asylum* on a case-by-case basis to aliens who are physically present in the United States or at a land border or port of entry and who meet the definition of a refugee.[4] After one year in refugee status in the United States, refugees are required to apply to adjust to legal permanent resident (LPR) status.[5]

REFUGEE ADMISSIONS

The United States aims to consider for resettlement at least half of the refugees referred by the United Nations High Commissioner for Refugees (UNHCR) for resettlement worldwide each year, depending on the availability of funding. By law, the annual number of refugee admissions and the allocation of these numbers by region of the world are set by the President after consultation with Congress.[6]

Each year, the President submits a report to the House of Representatives and the Senate, known as the *consultation document*, which contains the Administration's proposed worldwide refugee ceiling and regional allocations for the upcoming fiscal year.[7]

Following congressional consultations on the Administration's proposal, the President issues a Presidential Determination setting the refugee numbers for that year.[8] Table 1 shows refugee admissions ceilings and regional allocations for FY2001-FY2012.

The U.S. refugee program was greatly impacted by the terrorist attacks of September 11, 2001. In the aftermath of those attacks, a review of refugee-related security procedures was undertaken, refugee admissions were briefly suspended, and enhanced security measures were implemented.

As a result of these and other factors, actual refugee admissions plunged, declining from an FY2001 total of 69,304 to an FY2002 total of 27,131 and an FY2003 total of 28,404, as shown in the last row of Table 1.[9]

Table 1. Refugee Admissions Ceilings and Regional Allocations, FY2001-FY2012

Region	FY2001	FY2002	FY2003	FY2004	FY2005	FY2006	FY2007	FY2008	FY2009	FY2010	FY2011	FY2012
Africa	20,000	22,000	20,000	30,000b	21,000[c]	20,000	22,000	16,000	12,000	15,500	15,000	12,000
East Asia	6,000	4,000	4,000	8,500[b]	13,000	15,000	16,000[d]	20,000	20,500[f]	18,000g	19,000	18,000
Europe and Central Asia[a]	37,000	26,000	16,500	13,000	15,500[c]	15,000	6,500	3,000	2,500	2,500	2,000	2,000
Latin America/Caribbean	3,000	3,000	2,500	3,500	7,000[c]	5,000	5,000	5,000[e]	5,500[f]	5,500g	5,500	5,500
Near East/									39,500[f]	38,000g	35,500	35,500
South Asia	10,000	15,000	7,000	3,000[b]	3,500[c]	5,000	9,000[d]	28,000				
Unallocated	4,000	—	20,000	12,000[b]	10,000[c]	10,000	11,500[d]	8,000[e]	—[f]	500	3,000	3,000
Total ceilings	80,000	70,000	70,000	70,000	70,000	70,000	70,000	80,000	80,000	80,000	80,000	76,000
Actual admissions	69,304	27,131	28,404	52,873	53,813	41,223	48,282	60,191	74,654	73,311	56,424	NA

Sources: For ceiling and allocation data: PD 2000-32, September 29, 2000; PD 02-04, November 21, 2001; PD 03-02, October 16, 2002; PD 2004-06, October 21, 2003; PD 2004-53, September 30, 2004; PD 2006-3, October 24, 2005; PD 2007-1, October 11, 2006; PD 2008-1, October 2, 2007; PD 2008-29, September 30, 2008; PD 2009- 32, September 30, 2009; PD 2011-02, October 8, 2010; PD 2011-17, September 30, 2011. U.S. Department of State, U.S. Department of Justice, and U.S. Department of Health and Human Services, *Proposed Refugee Admissions* ... , Fiscal Years 2001-2012. For actual admissions data: U.S. Department of State, Bureau of Population, Refugees and Migration.

[a] For FY2001-FY2003, separate sub-allocations were provided for the former Yugoslavia and the Former Soviet Union (FSU); they are combined here.

[b] Of the FY2004 ceiling of 70,000, 50,000 numbers were originally allocated by region and 20,000 were unallocated. The unallocated reserve was tapped during the year to provide 8,000 additional numbers to Africa, East Asia, and Near East/South Asia.

[c] Of the FY2005 ceiling of 70,000, 50,000 numbers were originally allocated by region and 20,000 were unallocated. The unallocated reserve was tapped during the year to provide 10,000 additional numbers to Africa, Europe and Central Asia, Latin America/Caribbean, and Near East/South Asia.

[d] Of the FY2007 ceiling of 70,000, 50,000 numbers were originally allocated by region and 20,000 were unallocated. The unallocated reserve was tapped during the year to provide 8,500 additional numbers to East Asia and Near East/South Asia.

[e] Of the FY2008 ceiling of 80,000, 70,000 numbers were originally allocated by region and 10,000 were unallocated. The unallocated reserve was tapped during the year to provide 2,000 additional numbers to Latin America/Caribbean.

[f] Of the FY2009 ceiling of 80,000, 75,000 numbers were originally allocated by region and 5,000 were unallocated. The unallocated reserve was tapped during the year to provide 5,000 additional numbers to East Asia, Latin America/Caribbean, and Near East/South Asia.

[g] Of the FY2010 ceiling of 80,000, 75,000 numbers were originally allocated by region and 5,000 were unallocated. The unallocated reserve was tapped during the year to provide 4,500 additional numbers to East Asia, Latin America/Caribbean, and Near East/South Asia.

Admissions have rebounded since FY2002 and FY2003, totaling over 70,000 in each of FY2009 and FY2010. As shown in Table 1, however, there was a significant drop in admissions between FY2010 and FY2011, when admissions totaled 56,424. The FY2012 consultation document, written during FY2011, attributed the FY2010-FY2011 decrease largely to new security requirements:

> [FY2011's] admissions total will be lower ... due largely to the introduction of additional security checks during the year, including pre-departure checks shortly before refugees travel to the U.S., instituted mid-year, that enhance the vetting of applicants against intelligence and law enforcement information. While these checks caused a slowdown in refugee arrivals, the checks reflect the Administration's commitment to conduct the most thorough checks possible to prevent dangerous individuals from gaining access to the United States through the refugee program. Arrival numbers began to rebound in June and July [of 2011] and we expect arrivals in FY2012 approaching the proposed ceiling.[10]

FY2012 Refugee Ceiling and Allocations

On September 30, 2011, President Obama signed the Presidential Determination setting the FY2012 worldwide refugee ceiling and regional levels.[11] As indicated in Table 1, the FY2012 ceiling is 76,000. The ceiling and allocations in the FY2012 Presidential Determination are identical to those in the FY2012 consultation document.

The FY2012 refugee ceiling of 76,000 includes 73,000 admissions numbers allocated among the regions of the world and an unallocated reserve of 3,000 numbers. An unallocated reserve is to be used if, and where, a need develops for refugee slots in excess of the allocated numbers. This has occurred in recent years, as detailed in Table 1.

Africa has been allocated 12,000 refugee admissions numbers for FY2012. The FY2011 allocation to the region was 15,000, and FY2011 admissions totaled just over half that number (7,685).[12] According to the FY2012 consultation document, the shortfall in FY2011 African refugee arrivals resulted from several factors, including "challenges related to finalizing individual security clearances; our inability to launch a significantly larger resettlement program for Darfur refugees in Chad due to host government opposition;" and a decrease in referrals to the U.S. refugee admissions program from UNHCR. For Africa, as for all regions, the FY2012 allocation is intended to cover previously approved refugees in the pipeline as well as new cases. FY2012 admissions are expected to come primarily from East and Southern Africa and to include Somalis, Congolese, and Eritreans, among others.

East Asia's FY2012 allocation is 18,000, compared to an FY2011 allocation of 19,000. FY2011 admissions totaled 17,367. FY2012 admissions are expected to consist primarily of Burmese refugees living in Thailand and Malaysia.

Europe and Central Asia have a combined FY2012 allocation of 2,000 refugee numbers, the same as in FY2011. In FY2011, admissions totaled 1,228. The 2012 allocation includes projected admissions of "Lautenberg Amendment" cases from the former Soviet Union (discussed below).

The FY2012 allocation for Latin America and the Caribbean is 5,500, the same as the FY2011 allocation. FY2011 admissions totaled 2,976. Cubans account for the vast majority of admissions from this region.

The Near East/South Asia FY2012 allocation is 35,500, the same as the FY2011 allocation. FY2011 admissions totaled 27,168. FY2012 admissions are expected to include Iraqis, Bhutanese, Iranians, Pakistanis, and Afghans.

Refugee Processing Priorities

DOS is responsible for overseas processing of refugees. Generally, it arranges for a nongovernmental organization (NGO), an international organization, or U.S. embassy contractors to manage a Resettlement Support Center (RSC) that assists in refugee processing. RSC staff conduct pre-screening interviews of prospective refugees and prepare cases for submission to USCIS, which handles refugee adjudications. Overseas refugee processing is conducted through a system of three priorities for admission. These priorities are separate and distinct from whether such persons qualify for refugee status.

Priority 1 covers refugees for whom resettlement seems to be the appropriate durable solution, who are referred to the U.S. refugee program by UNHCR, a U.S. embassy, or a designated NGO. Such persons often have compelling protection needs, and may be in danger of attack or of being returned to the country they fled. All nationalities are eligible for this priority.

Priority 2 covers groups of special humanitarian concern to the United States. It includes specific groups that may be defined by their nationalities, clans, ethnicities, or other characteristics. Some of these groups, such as

Cuban dissidents and certain former Soviet nationals ("Lautenberg Amendment" cases, discussed below), are processed in their country of origin. Other Priority 2 groups are processed outside their country of origin. These include Iranian religious minorities ("Specter Amendment" cases, discussed below) processed in Austria and Turkey, and Burmese in refugee camps in Thailand. Unlike Priority 1 cases, individuals falling under Priority 2 are able to access the U.S. refugee program without a UNHCR, embassy, or NGO referral.

Priority 3 covers family reunification cases. Refugee applications under Priority 3 are based upon an *affidavit of relationship* (AOR) filed by an eligible relative in the United States. The Priority 3 program, which is limited to designated nationalties, has changed over the years. [13] Since FY2004, it has comprised cases of spouses, unmarried children under age 21, and parents of persons who were admitted to the United States as refugees or granted asylum. Individuals falling under Priority 3, like those falling under Priority 2, are able to access the U.S. refugee program without a UNHCR, embassy, or NGO referral.

On October 22, 2008, the U.S. refugee program stopped accepting applications under Priority 3.[14] Earlier in 2008, processing of Priority 3 cases was suspended in certain locations in Africa "due to indications of extremely high rates of fraud obtained through pilot DNA testing."[15] A revised Priority 3 program is under consideration. According to the FY2012 consultation document:

> PRM and DHS/USCIS will update the Congress when the revisions [to the P-3 program and AOR] are complete, and we are prepared to resume P-3 processing, likely with a DNA relationship testing requirement for certain claimed biological relationships.[16]

Upon resumption, Priority 3 processing will be available to nationals of 20 countries.[17]

Refugee Adjudications

USCIS is responsible for adjudicating refugee cases. It makes determinations about whether an individual qualifies for refugee status and is otherwise admissible to the United States. In the past, the majority of refugee adjudications were conducted by USCIS officers on temporary duty from domestic asylum offices. Today, these adjudications are handled by USCIS officers in the Refugee Corps.

Admissibility of Refugees

In order to be admitted to the United States, a prospective refugee must be *admissible* under immigration law. The INA sets forth various grounds of inadmissibility, which include health-related grounds, security-related grounds, public charge (i.e., indigence), and lack of proper documentation.[18] Some inadmissibility grounds (public charge, lack of proper documentation) are not applicable to refugees. Others can be waived for humanitarian purposes, to assure family unity, or when it is otherwise in the public interest.[19] Of particular relevance to the admission of refugees are certain health-related and security-related grounds of inadmissibility.

Under the INA health-related grounds of inadmissibility, an alien who is determined, in accordance with Department of Health and Human Services (HHS) regulations, to have a communicable disease of public health significance is inadmissible. Until recently, human immunodeficiency virus (HIV) infection was defined to be one of these diseases, although HIV-infected refugees could apply for a waiver. In 2008, Congress amended the INA to eliminate the reference to HIV infection as a health-related ground of inadmissibility.[20] And effective January 4, 2010, the Centers for Disease Control and Prevention (CDC) of HHS amended its regulations to remove HIV infection from the definition of a communicable disease of public health significance.[21]

Since 1990, the security-related grounds of inadmissibility in the INA have expressly included terrorism-related grounds. Over the years, the terrorism-related grounds have been amended to lower the threshold for how substantial, apparent, and immediate an alien's support for a terrorist activity or organization may be for the alien to be rendered inadmissible.[22] Among the current terrorism-related grounds, an alien is generally inadmissible for engaging in terrorist activity if he or she gives any material support, such as a safe house, transportation, communications, or funds, to a terrorist organization or any of its members or to a person engaged in terrorist activity. The Secretary of State or the Secretary of DHS, after consultation with the other and the Attorney General, may exercise discretionary waiver authority over certain terrorism-related grounds of inadmissibility. Both the Secretary of State and the Secretary of DHS have exercised this waiver authority with respect to certain categories of individuals.

The Consolidated Appropriations Act, 2008, enacted in December 2007, specifies groups that, for purposes of the INA terrorism-related grounds of inadmissibility, are not to be considered terrorist organizations on the basis of past acts. [23] Thus, a prospective refugee who provided support to one of these groups would not be subject to the material support inadmissibility provision on the basis of those actions. More broadly, the Consolidated Appropriations Act expands the discretionary authority of the Secretary of State and the Secretary of DHS to grant waivers of the terrorism-related grounds of inadmissibility generally.

Special Refugee Provisions

Lautenberg Amendment and Specter Amendment

The "Lautenberg Amendment" is a provision of the FY1990 Foreign Operations Appropriations Act. It requires the Attorney General to designate categories of former Soviet and Indochinese nationals for whom less evidence is needed to prove refugee status, and provides for adjustment to permanent resident status of certain Soviet and Indochinese nationals granted parole after being denied refugee status.[24]

Applicants for refugee status under the special provision are required to prove that they are members of a protected category with a credible, but not necessarily individual, fear of persecution. By contrast, the INA requires prospective refugees to establish a well-founded fear of persecution on a case-by-case basis.

The Lautenberg Amendment has been regularly extended in appropriations acts, although there have often been gaps between extensions. The Consolidated Appropriations Act, 2004, in addition to extending the amendment through FY2004, amended the Lautenberg Amendment to add a new provision known as the "Specter Amendment."[25] The Specter Amendment requires the designation of categories of Iranian nationals, specifically religious minorities, for whom less evidence is needed to prove refugee status.

The Consolidated Appropriations Act, 2010, extended the Lautenberg Amendment, including the Specter Amendment, through FY2010.[26] For FY2011, Congress extended the amendment only until June 1, 2011,[27] and it temporarily lapsed on that date. It was re-enacted for FY2012[28] and is now in effect until October 1, 2012.

Vietnamese Refugees

The "McCain Amendment" was first enacted in the FY1997 Omnibus Consolidated Appropriations Act.[29] It covered certain adult children, whose parents were Vietnamese reeducation camp survivors and had been accepted for U.S. refugee resettlement. The amendment made the adult children eligible for U.S. refugee resettlement. It was subsequently amended and extended through FY1999.

In November 1999, the McCain Amendment was re-enacted in revised form for FY2000 and FY2001 in the Consolidated Appropriations Act, 2000.[30] As revised, it applied to the adult children of a re-education camp survivor who was residing in the United States or awaiting departure from Vietnam and who, after April 1995, was accepted for U.S. refugee resettlement or for admission as an immediate relative immigrant. The April 1995 date restriction did not apply to children who were previously denied refugee resettlement because their documents did not show continuous co-residency with their parent.

Legislation to amend and extend the provision through FY2003 was approved by the 107th Congress in May 2002.[31] This law eliminated the existing April 1995 date restriction. Thus, children who were previously denied refugee resettlement for reasons other than co-residency could also have their cases reconsidered. This revised provision, which was regularly extended,[32] is sometimes referred to as the "McCain-Davis Amendment." The McCain-Davis Amendment was last extended, through FY2010, by the Omnibus Appropriations Act, 2009.[33] This extension was repealed, however, by the Consolidated Appropriations Act, 2010,[34] and the McCain amendment is no longer in effect.

REFUGEE RESETTLEMENT ASSISTANCE

The Department of Health and Human Service's Office of Refugee Resettlement (HHS/ORR), within the Administration for Children and Families, administers an initial transitional assistance program for temporarily dependent refugees and Cuban/Haitian entrants. Since its establishment in 1980, the refugee resettlement program has been justified on the grounds that the admission of refugees is a federal decision, entailing some federal responsibility. Unlike immigrants who enter through family or employment ties, refugees are admitted on humanitarian grounds, and there is no requirement that they demonstrate economic self-sufficiency.

Table 2. Refugee Resettlement Funding, FY2003-FY2012 (budget authority in millions)

Programs	FY03 enacted	FY04 actual	FY05 actual	FY06 actual	FY07 enacted	FY08 enacted[f]	FY09 estimate	FY10 enacted	FY11 enacted	FY12 enacted
Transitional/Cash and Medical Services	$219.9	$169.0	$205.0	$265.4	$265.5	$301.3	$282.3	$353.3	$352.6	$372.3
Victims of Trafficking[a]	9.9	9.9	9.9	9.8	9.8	10.0	9.8	9.8	9.8	9.8
Social Services	150.1	152.2	152.2	153.9	154.0	156.7	154.0	154.0	153.7	153.4
Victims of Torture[b]	9.9	9.9	9.9	9.8	9.8	10.0	10.8	11.1	11.1	11.0
Preventive Health	4.8	4.8	4.8	4.7	4.7	4.8	4.7	4,7	4,7	4,7
Targeted Assistance	49.2	49.0	49.1	48.6	48.6	49.5	48.6	48.6	48.5	48.4
Unaccompanied Alien Children[c]	37.1[e]	52.8	53.8	77.2	95.3	135.0	123.1	149.4	149.1	168.7
Total[d]	$480.9	$447.6	$484.7	$569.4	$587.8	$667.3	$633.4	$730.9	$729.5	$768.3

Sources: U.S. Department of Health and Human Services, Administration for Children and Families, *Justifications of Estimates for Appropriations Committees*, Fiscal Years 2005-2013; U.S. Department of Health and Human Services, Administration for Children and Families, "Administration for Children and Families 2005-2007 All-Purpose Table"; U.S. Congress, Conference Committees, *Departments of Transportation and Housing and Urban Development, and Related Agencies Appropriations Act, 2010*, conference report to accompany H.R. 3288, 111th Cong., 1st sess., H.Rept. 111-366, Labor-Health and Human Services-Education funding table, p. 1292.

[a] Funding used primarily for administrative cost of certifying that an alien is a trafficking victim for purposes of receiving benefits and services.

[b] Funding used for rehabilitation services, social services, and legal services for torture victims and for provision of research and training to health care providers.

[c] The Homeland Security Act of 2002 (P.L. 107-296) transferred functions under U.S. immigration law related to the care of unaccompanied alien children from the then-INS to HHS/ORR.

[d] Sum of listed amounts may not equal total due to rounding.

[e] This funding was transferred to ORR from the former INS, pursuant to P.L. 107-296.

[f] Amounts do not reflect the required 1.747% recision.

For FY2012, appropriations for ORR refugee assistance totaled $768.3 million. Table 2 details refugee resettlement funding for FY2003-FY2012. For FY2013, the President has requested $805.4 million for refugee assistance.

ORR-funded refugee assistance activities include refugee cash and medical assistance, social services to help refugees become socially and economically self-sufficient, and targeted assistance for impacted areas. Special refugee cash assistance (RCA) and refugee medical assistance (RMA) are the heart of the refugee program, accounting for a greater portion of the ORR annual budget than any other activity (see **Table 2**). RCA and RMA, which in most cases are administered by the states, are intended to help needy refugees who are ineligible to receive benefits from mainstream federal assistance programs. RCA and RMA are currently available to refugees for eight months after entry.[35] RMA benefits are based on the state's Medicaid program, and RCA payments are now based on the state's Temporary Assistance for Needy Families (TANF) payment to a family unit of the same size.[36]

The ORR program was significantly affected by the 1996 welfare reform act and subsequent amendments.[37] Prior to this legislation, refugees who otherwise met the requirements of federal public assistance programs were immediately and indefinitely eligible to participate in them just like U.S. citizens. Now, refugees and other specified humanitarian entrants are subject to time limits. Table 3 summarizes the time limits on refugee eligibility for four major public assistance programs.

Table 3. Refugee Eligibility for Major Federal Public Assistance Programs

Program	Eligibility
Supplemental Security Income (SSI) for the Aged, Blind and Disabled	Eligible for seven years after entry.a
Medicaid (non-emergency care)	Eligible for seven years after entry, then state option.
TANF	Eligible for five years after entry, then state option.
Supplemental Nutrition Assistance Program (SNAP) (formerly, Food Stamps)	Eligible without time limits.

a. A temporary provision (in P.L. 110-328, September 30, 2008) extended to nine years (during FY2009 through FY2011) the period of eligibility of certain refugees and others for SSI benefits, provided that specified criteria were met.

APPENDIX: REFUGEE ADMISSIONS BY REGION, FY1987-FY2011

FY	Africa	East Asia	Eastern Europe	Former Soviet Union	Latin America/ Caribbean	Near East/ South Asia	Total
1987	1,990	40,099	8,396	3,699	323	10,021	**64,528**
1988	1,593	35,371	7,510	20,411	3,230[a]	8,368	**76,483**
1989	1,902	45,722	8,752	39,602	4,116[a]	6,976[a]	**107,070**
1990	3,453	51,604[a]	6,094	50,628	5,308[a]	4,979	**122,066**
1991	4,420	53,522	6,837	39,226	4,042[a]	5,342	**113,389**
1992	5,470	51,899	2,915	61,397	3,947[a]	6,903	**132,531**
1993	6,967	49,817	2,582	48,773	4,322[a]	6,987	**119,448**
1994	5,860	43,564	7,707	43,854	6,156	5,840	**112,981**
1995	4,827	36,987	10,070	35,951	7,629	4,510	**99,974**
1996	7,604	19,321	12,145	29,816	3,550	3,967	**76,403**
1997	6,065	8,594	21,401	27,331	2,996	4,101	**70,488**
1998	6,887	10,854	30,842	23,557	1,627	3,313	**77,080**
1999	13,043	10,206	38,658	17,410	2,110	4,098	**85,525**
2000	17,561	4,561	22,561	15,103	3,232	10,129	**73,147**
2001	19,021	3,725	15,777	15,748	2,973	12,060	**69,304**
2002	2,551	3,512	5,459	9,969	1,934	3,706	**27,131**
2003	10,715	1,724	2,506	8,744	455	4,260	**28,404**
2004	29,104	8,084	9,254[b]		3,577	2,854	**52,873**
2005	20,745	12,076	11,316[b]		6,699	2,977	**53,813**
2006	18,126	5,659	10,456[b]		3,264	3,718	**41,223**
2007	17,483	15,643	4,560[b]		2,976	7,620	**48,282**
2008	8,935	19,489	2,343[b]		4,277	25,147	**60,191**
2009	9,670	19,850	1,997[b]		4,857	38,280	**74,654**
2010	13,305	17,716	1,526[b]		4,982	35,782	**73,311**
2011	7,685	17,367	1,228[b]		2,976	27,168	**56,424**

Source: U.S. Department of State, Bureau of Population, Refugees and Migration.

Notes: Data for 2002-2011 are as of February 29, 2012. Data for earlier years may not reflect all subsequent adjustments.

[a] Includes refugees admitted under the Private Sector Initiative (PSI), most of whom were Cuban.

[b] Beginning in FY2004, the categories of Eastern Europe and the Former Soviet Union were combined into a single category, Europe and Central Asia. These are the total admissions under that category.

End Notes

[1] The INA is Act of June 27, 1952, ch. 477, codified, as amended, at 8 U.S.C. §§1101 *et seq.* The Refugee Act is P.L. 96-212, March 17, 1980.

[2] This definition conforms with the definition used in the United Nations Convention and Protocol relating to the status of refugees.

[3] INA §101(a)(42).

[4] For further information on asylum, see CRS Report R41753, *Asylum and "Credible Fear" Issues in U.S. Immigration Policy*, by Ruth Ellen Wasem.

[5] INA §209(a). Asylees (those granted asylum) may apply for LPR status after one year, but are not required to do so. There are no numerical limitations on refugee or asylee adjustments of status.

[6] INA §207(a).

[7] The consultation document for FY2012 is U.S. Department of State, U.S. Department of Homeland Security, and U.S. Department of Health and Human Services, *Proposed Refugee Admissions for Fiscal Year 2012: Report to the Congress*, http://www.state.gov/documents/organization/181378.pdf. (Hereinafter cited as *Proposed Refugee Admissions for Fiscal Year 2012.*)

[8] Asylees are not included in the refugee ceiling. There are no numerical limitations on the granting of asylum.

[9] Refugee admissions had not been at or below the FY2002 or FY2003 levels since FY1977, when admissions totaled about 20,000. From FY1979 through FY2001, annual refugee admissions totaled more than 60,000. For annual data on refugee admissions by region since FY1987, see the Appendix at the end of this report.

[10] *Proposed Refugee Admissions for Fiscal Year 2012*, p. iv.

[11] U.S. President [Obama], "Fiscal Year 2012 Refugee Admissions Numbers and Authorizations of In-Country Refugee Status ...," Presidential Determination No. 2011-17 of September 30, 2011, 76 *Federal Register*, pp. 62597-62598, October 11, 2011.

[12] See Appendix for annual refugee admissions numbers by region since FY1987.

[13] The number of nationalities eligible for Priority 3 processing has varied in recent years. During the late 1990s, the State Department found that a large number of Priority 3 applications were received from persons who did not qualify for refugee status and that there was a significant amount of fraud associated with these applications. To address these problems, the U.S. government reduced the number of nationalities eligible for such refugee slots. For FY2003, four nationalities were eligible for Priority 3 processing. For FY2004, the Priority 3 program was revised on a pilot basis. To simultaneously broaden access to the program and continue to address concerns about fraud, the number of eligible nationalities was increased to nine, while the types of qualifying relationships were restricted. As noted above, eligibility for Priority 3 currently requires a qualifying relationship with an individual who was admitted to the United States as a refugee or granted asylum. Prior to FY2004, this processing priority was available to those with qualifying relationships with a much wider range of legal U.S. residents without regard to how these residents gained admission to the United States. In another change, since FY2004, children have to be under age 21 to be eligible for Priority 3. In the past, this processing priority was also available to older unmarried sons and daughters. These changes to the Priority 3 qualifying relationships have remained in place since FY2004.

[14] U.S. Department of State, Bureau of Population, Refugees, and Migration, "Fraud in the Refugee Family Reunification (Priority Three) Program," fact sheet, December 4, 2008.

[15] *Proposed Refugee Admissions for Fiscal Year 2012*, p. 12.

[16] Ibid.

[17] The countries are Afghanistan, Bhutan, Burma, Burundi, Central African Republic, Chad, Colombia, Cuba, Democratic People's Republic of Korea (DPRK), Democratic Republic of Congo (DRC), Eritrea, Ethiopia, Iran, Iraq, Republic of Congo (ROC), Somalia, Sri Lanka, Sudan, Uzbekistan, and Zimbabwe. *Proposed Refugee Admissions for Fiscal Year 2012*, pp. 12-13.

[18] For further information on the grounds of inadmissibility generally, see CRS Report R41104, *Immigration Visa Issuances and Grounds for Exclusion: Policy and Trends*, by Ruth Ellen Wasem.

[19] Certain grounds of inadmissibility, including most security-related grounds, cannot be waived.

[20] P.L. 110-293, Title III, §305, July 30, 2008.

[21] U.S. Department of Health and Human Services, Centers for Disease Control and Prevention, "Medical Examination of Aliens—Removal of Human Immunodeficiency Virus (HIV) Infection From Definition of Communicable Disease of Public Health Significance," 74 *Federal Register*, pp. 56547-56562, November 2, 2009.

[22] See CRS Report RL32564, *Immigration: Terrorist Grounds for Exclusion and Removal of Aliens*, by Michael John Garcia and Ruth Ellen Wasem.

[23] P.L. 110-161, Division J, Title VI, §691, December 26, 2007. DHS and DOS followed this enactment with a series of *Federal Register* notices similarly stating that the terrorism-related grounds of inadmissibility would generally be waived with respect to any assistance provided by an alien to any of the entities expressly exempted by the Consolidated Appropriations Act, 2008, from being deemed terrorist organizations. U.S. Department of Homeland Security, Office of the Secretary, and Department of State, Office of the Secretary, "Exercise of Authority Under Section 212(d)(3)(B)(i) of the Immigration and Nationality Act" [10 separate notices with same title], 73 *Federal Register* 34770-34777, June 18, 2008.

[24] P.L. 101-167, Title V, §599D and §599E, November 21, 1989. Parole is a temporary authorization to enter the United States and is typically granted when the alien's entry is determined to be in the public interest.

[25] P.L. 108-199, Division E, Title II, §213, January 23, 2004.

[26] P.L. 111-117, Division F, Title VII, §7034(f), December 16, 2009. Earlier extensions were included in P.L. 108-447, December 8, 2004; P.L. 109-102, November 14, 2005; P.L. 110-5, February 15, 2007; and P.L. 110-161, December 26, 2007.

[27] P.L. 112-10, Division B, §2121(m), April 15, 2011.

[28] P.L. 112-74, Division I, §7034(r), December 23, 2011.

[29] Section 584 of P.L. 104-208, Division A, Section 101(c), September 30, 1996.

[30] P.L. 106-113, Appendix G, Division A, §255, November 29, 1999.

[31] P.L. 107-185, May 30, 2002.

[32] It was extended by P.L. 108-447, P.L. 109-102, and P.L. 110-161.

[33] P.L. 111-8, Division H, §7034(d), March 11, 2009.

[34] P.L. 111-117, Division F, §7034(d).

[35] INA §412(e)(1) authorizes ORR to reimburse states for RCA and RMA for 36 months. Initially, beginning in April 1980, RCA and RMA were available for the full 36 months. As appropriations levels decreased in subsequent years, however, the period of coverage was reduced. Since October 1991, RCA and RMA have been available to refugees for eight months after entry.

[36] For additional discussion of ORR assistance, see CRS Report R41570, *U.S. Refugee Resettlement Assistance*, by Andorra Bruno.

[37] The 1996 welfare reform law is the Personal Responsibility and Work Opportunity Reconciliation Act, P.L. 104-193, August 22, 1996.

In: Refugee Resettlement in the United States ISBN: 978-1-62257-962-4
Editors: R. J. Irvin and L. Gambrell

Chapter 2

U.S. Refugee Resettlement Assistance*

Andorra Bruno

Summary

In recent years, the United States has admitted an increasingly diverse group of refugees and other humanitarian cases with a diverse set of needs. There seems to be broad consensus that the U.S. refugee resettlement assistance system is not adequately meeting the needs of these new arrivals and is ripe for reform. The National Security Council is leading an interagency review of refugee resettlement, the forthcoming results of which may further energize reform efforts. To help inform possible future efforts to reform the refugee resettlement assistance system, this report discusses existing resettlement assistance programs, key challenges and issues in providing effective assistance, and policy options to reform the current system.

To assist newly arriving refugees, the Department of State (DOS) administers a program of initial resettlement known as the Reception and Placement Program. Under this program, public and private, nonprofit entities provide new refugees with initial resettlement services and referrals to other services, as needed.

* This is an edited, reformatted and augmented version of a Congressional Research Service publiccation, CRS Report for Congress R41570, from www.crs.gov, dated January 4, 2011.

A separate set of refugee resettlement assistance programs, administered by the Office of Refugee Resettlement (ORR) in the Department of Health and Human Services' Administration for Children and Families (HHS/ACF), provides transitional assistance to refugees and other designated groups. These groups include individuals granted asylum, Cuban and Haitian entrants, trafficking victims, Amerasians, and Iraqi and Afghan special immigrants. The ORR programs— which provide mainly cash assistance, medical assistance, and employment-related services—are intended to help the beneficiaries (who are referred to collectively as "refugees" in this report) achieve economic self-sufficiency as soon as possible after their arrival in the United States.

Many observers argue that the DOS and ORR programs and the refugee resettlement assistance system more broadly are in need of reform. A number of reports have identified perceived shortcomings in the existing system and have offered recommendations for change. Several of these reports have focused, in particular, on the recent experience of Iraqi refugees resettled in the United States.

Among the broad challenges facing the refugee resettlement assistance system are interagency coordination and information sharing, and funding. Critics also question the system's self-sufficiency model, which requires refugees to secure employment as quickly as possible. Key issues include financial assistance to refugees, which is widely viewed as insufficient, and the "lottery effect," whereby refugees resettled in different parts of the United States receive different levels of financial assistance and services. Growing out of these challenges and issues are a variety of options for reforming the existing system with respect to administration and planning and the ORR programs.

INTRODUCTION

In the early years of the [refugee] program, large numbers of relatively few nationalities located in a limited number of countries dominated the program. Many of the resettled refugees had family members already in the United States. Over the past decade, however, the United States has worked closely with the United Nations High Commissioner for Refugees (UNHCR) to make third country resettlement a viable, durable solution for increasing numbers from a broader representation of the world's refugee population, which currently stands at over 10 million. While we have again resettled large numbers of Iraqis, Burmese, and Bhutanese this year, the USRAP has admitted refugees from over 60 nationalities who were processed in some 90 countries. Over 80 percent of these applicants were referred to us by UNHCR either individually or in groups. Relatively few have family members resident in the United States.

> The Administration has worked closely with the Congress to invest the resources necessary to reach smaller numbers of the most desperate populations who find themselves in seemingly forgotten locations. 1

This excerpt, from the interagency report *Proposed Refugee Admissions for FY2011*, suggests the extent of the challenge facing the U.S. government as it resettles a diverse group of individuals with a wide range of needs. A set of refugee resettlement assistance programs, administered by the Office of Refugee Resettlement (ORR) in the Department of Health and Human Services' Administration for Children and Families (HHS/ACF), provides transitional assistance to refugees and other designated groups. These programs are intended to help the beneficiaries (who are referred to collectively as "refugees" in this report) achieve economic self-sufficiency as soon as possible after their arrival in the United States. Achievement of self-sufficiency has been more difficult in recent years in the face of the economic recession. In light of the economic situation and obstacles to employment facing arriving refugees, HHS requested additional ORR funding for FY2011.

Separate from the ORR program, the Department of State (DOS) administers a program of initial resettlement for newly arriving refugees known as the Reception and Placement Program. Under this program, public and private, nonprofit entities provide arriving refugees with initial resettlement services and referrals to other services, as needed. To provide the required services, the participating agencies use Reception and Placement Program funds and contributions from other sources. In 2010, DOS increased the Reception and Placement grant provided to these agencies from $900 to $1,800 per refugee.

These recent steps by HHS and DOS to provide additional resources for refugee resettlement reflect a larger view on the part of many observers that the refugee resettlement assistance system is in need of reform. The Obama Administration has initiated an interagency review of refugee resettlement, which is being lead by the National Security Council (NSC). There is little public information about the review. A June 2010 article in the *Los Angeles Times* described it as "the first thorough review of refugee resettlement in 30 years," and reported that the NSC had consulted with federal agencies, including HHS and DOS, and refugee advocates.[2]

It is not known when the results of the review will be made available. They have been widely anticipated, however, and may further energize reform efforts.

To help inform possible future efforts to reform the refugee resettlement assistance system, this report discusses existing resettlement assistance programs, key issues and challenges in providing effective assistance, and policy options to reform the current system. While the refugee admissions process is briefly described and referenced in parts of this report, as relevant, the focus of this report is on resettlement assistance to refugees in the United States.

Background on Refugee Admissions and Resettlement Policy

The admission of refugees to the United States and their resettlement here are authorized by the Immigration and Nationality Act (INA), as amended by the Refugee Act of 1980.[3] Refugees are one of the main categories of foreign nationals admitted on humanitarian grounds to live permanently in the United States. Humanitarian admissions represent one stream of permanent admissions under U.S. immigration law.[4]

The INA, as amended, sets forth procedures for determining refugee admissions levels and criteria for admitting refugees to the United States.[5] It also requires refugees to apply to adjust to legal permanent resident (LPR) status after one year in refugee status in the United States.

In addition to establishing admissions procedures, the INA, as amended by the Refugee Act of 1980, authorizes federal assistance to resettle refugees and promote their self-sufficiency. It authorizes several refugee assistance programs, as discussed below. The Refugee Act of 1980 also amended the INA to establish ORR at HHS to administer the refugee assistance programs. Refugee assistance programs are not limited to individuals who are admitted to the United States as refugees. Rather, as detailed below, refugee assistance and benefits are available to various categories of humanitarian admissions.

Groups Eligible for Refugee Resettlement Assistance and Benefits

The following groups are eligible, by law, for certain types of refugee resettlement assistance:

- Refugees
  Under the INA, a refugee is a person who is outside his or her country and who is unable or unwilling to return to, and is unable or unwilling to avail himself or herself of the protection of, that country because of persecution or a well-founded fear of persecution on account of race, religion, nationality, membership in a particular social group, or political opinion. In special circumstances, a refugee may also be a person who is within his or her country and who is persecuted or has a well-founded fear of persecution on account of race, religion, nationality, membership in a particular social group, or political opinion. Excluded from the definition of a refugee is any person who participated in the persecution of another.[6]
- Asylees
  An alien in the United States or at a port of entry who establishes that he or she is a refugee under the INA, as defined above, may be granted asylum. A person granted asylum is referred to as an asylee.[7]
- Cuban and Haitian Entrants
  A Cuban and Haitian entrant is (1) any individual granted parole status as a Cuban/ Haitian Entrant (Status Pending) or granted any other special status subsequently established under the immigration laws for nationals of Cuba or Haiti, regardless of the status of the individual at the time assistance or services are provided; and (2) any other national of Cuba or Haiti (A) who (i) was paroled into the United States and has not acquired any other status under the INA; (ii) is the subject of removal proceedings under the INA; or (iii) has an asylum application pending; and (B) with respect to whom a final, nonappealable, and legally enforceable order of removal has not been entered.[8]
- Trafficking Victims
  A victim of a severe form of trafficking in persons is a person who has been subjected to a severe form of trafficking as set forth in P.L. 106-386, such as sex trafficking, and who either (1) is under age 18 or

(2) is an adult who obtains certification from the Secretary of Health and Human Services.[9]

- Amerasians

  An Amerasian is an alien who, as of December 22, 1987, is residing in Vietnam and who establishes to the satisfaction of a consular officer or an Immigration and Naturalization Service (INS) officer that the alien (1) was born in Vietnam after January 1, 1962, and before January 1, 1976, and was fathered by a citizen of the United States (referred to as a "principal alien"); (2) is the spouse or child of a principal alien and is accompanying, or following to join, the principal alien; or (3) is subject to further requirements, either (A) is the principal alien's natural mother (or is the spouse or child of such mother), or (B) has acted in effect as the principal alien's mother, father, or next-of-kin (or is the spouse or child of such an alien), and is accompanying, or following to join, the principal alien.[10]
- Iraqi and Afghan Special Immigrants

  Iraqis and Afghans are admitted to the United States as legal permanent residents (LPRs) under several special immigrant programs. One of these programs, known as the Section 1059 program for the provision that established it, authorizes DHS to grant LPR status to certain nationals of Iraq and Afghanistan who have worked directly with the U.S. Armed Forces, or under Chief of Mission authority, as translators or interpreters.[11] Another special immigrant program, known as the Section 1244 program, covers Iraqi nationals who are or were employed by or on behalf of the U.S. government in Iraq on or after March 20, 2003, for not less than one year; provided documented valuable service to the U.S. government; and have experienced "an ongoing serious threat" as a result of their employment by the U.S. government."[12] A parallel special immigrant program for Afghans covers nationals of Afghanistan who are or were employed by or on behalf of the U.S. government in Afghanistan on or after October 7, 2001, for not less than one year; provided documented valuable service to the U.S. government; and have experienced "an ongoing serious threat" as a result of their employment.[13]

Changes in the Refugee Program Over Time

As noted above, the resettlement assistance system seeks to promote the rapid economic adjustment and self-sufficiency of refugees. During the 30 years since the establishment of the current refugee resettlement assistance programs in 1980, there have been many developments that have affected the ability of refugees to achieve self-sufficiency. These developments include changes in the refugee population and in the resettlement assistance programs as well as other policy shifts and broader economic developments. This section highlights selected changes during the last 30 years that are relevant to the economic adjustment of refugees.

Selected Characteristics at Time of Arrival

Since the early years of the U.S. refugee program, data related to economic adjustment, including data on educational background and English language proficiency, have been collected about refugees in the United States. Education and English language ability, among other factors, affect the employment prospects of refugees. Table 1 shows data on average years of education and English language ability at the time of U.S. entry that were self-reported by refugees in annual surveys. These surveys were restricted to Southeast Asian refugees prior to 1993. In 1982 and 1986, the first two years of entry listed in Table 1, Southeast Asian refugees from Cambodia, Laos, and Vietnam accounted for about 75% and about 70%, respectively, of total annual refugee arrivals according to data from the former Immigration and Naturalization Service.[14] Thus, while caution must be taken in drawing conclusions from Table 1 in light of the changes in the survey population and the self-reporting of the data, the data may generally suggest that compared to refugees arriving in the early years of the U.S. refugee program, arrivals in more recent years have had more education but less English language ability.

Availability of Refugee Resettlement Assistance and Economic Changes

Over the years, policymakers have made changes to refugee eligibility for public assistance. As explained below, needy refugees who do not meet all the eligibility requirements for certain federal public assistance programs may receive special refugee cash assistance and refugee medical assistance. When the refugee assistance program was first established in 1980, refugee cash assistance and medical assistance were available for up to 36 months. Since 1991, these forms of assistance have been limited to eight months. Some observers have pointed to the availability of 36 months of cash assistance as a contributing factor to the long-term economic success of Vietnamese refugees, who arrived in large numbers in the 1980s.[15] Reforms to major federal assistance programs during the past 20 years, which in some cases have included the tightening of eligibility requirements and the limiting of benefits for noncitizens generally, have likewise impacted refugees.[16]

Accompanying these various changes in refugee eligibility for different forms of public assistance have been changes in the economy. Economic fluctuations, particularly those that affect the availability of jobs, can have a profound effect on the ability of refugees to successfully resettle in the United States.

Table 1. Education and English Language Ability of Refugees at Time of U.S. Entry: Selected Years

Year of Entry	Average Number of Years of Education	Percentage Speaking No English
1982[a]	6.8	42%
1986[a]	4.9	46%
1990-1995[b]	10.5	59%
1996-2001[b]	10.9	60%
2002-2007[b]	9.1	58%

Sources: U.S. Department of Health and Human Services, Social Security Administration, Office of Refugee Resettlement, *Refugee Resettlement Program*, Report to the Congress, January 31, 1983; U.S. Department of Health and Human Services, Family Support Administration, Office of Refugee Resettlement, *Refugee Resettlement Program*, Report to the Congress, January 31, 1987; U.S. Department of Health and Human Services, Administration for Children and Families, Office of Refugee Resettlement, *Refugee Resettlement Program*, Report to the Congress, FY1995, FY2001; U.S. Department of Health and Human Services, Administration for Children and Families, Office of Refugee Resettlement, *Office of Refugee Resettlement*, Report to the Congress, FY2007.

Notes: All data are self-reported by refugees about their circumstances when they first arrived in the United States. Data for years prior to 1993 are restricted to Southeast Asian refugees. Data for 1986 and later years are for refugees ages 16 or above.

[a] Data for 1982 and 1986 are limited to Southeast Asian refugees.

[b] Data are averages for these years.

REFUGEE RESETTLEMENT ASSISTANCE PROGRAMS

The INA authorizes several refugee assistance programs, including an initial resettlement program cash and medical assistance, and a program to provide employment-related and other services.[17] ORR programs for refugee minors, non-refugee unaccompanied alien children, survivors of torture, and victims of trafficking are not covered in this report.[18]

DOS Reception and Placement Program

In authorizing a program for the initial resettlement of refugees, the Refugee Act of 1980 gave the President the authority to determine whether ORR or another office should administer the program, which had previously been the responsibility of DOS. President Jimmy Carter subsequently determined that DOS should retain administration of this program, known as the Reception and Placement Program.[19]

The Reception and Placement Program primarily serves aliens who are admitted to the United States as refugees. Iraqi and Afghan special immigrants may also receive benefits under this program if they elect to receive them during the special immigrant visa application process. In order to receive DOS benefits under the Reception and Placement Program, however, special immigrants must accept all of the associated benefits. These benefits include having their travel to the United States arranged by the International Organization for Migration (IOM), the organization that makes travel arrangements for refugees.

Under the Reception and Placement Program, DOS's Bureau of Population, Refugees, and Migration (PRM) funds cooperative agreements with public and private, nonprofit entities to provide initial services to refugees. These entities, referred to as voluntary agencies (or volags), maintain nationwide networks of local affiliates to provide services.[20] These services include pre-arrival services (e.g., placement); reception upon arrival in the United States; basic needs support (e.g., housing, furnishings, food, and clothing) for at least 30 days; and referrals to health, employment, education, and other services, as needed.

With respect to placement, the ORR director and the agency administering the Reception and Placement Program are required by law to "consult regularly ... with State and local governments and private nonprofit voluntary agencies concerning ... the intended distribution of refugees among the States and localities."[21] The ORR director is further directed to develop and implement, in consultation with voluntary agencies and state and local governments, policies for the placement and resettlement of refugees in the United States.

As part of PRM's annual Reception and Placement Program request for grant proposals, currently participating voluntary agencies and new applicants are required to provide data and narrative information about the agency and its affiliates. As in past years, proposals for FY2011 had to contain abstracts about existing or proposed affiliates that included, among other required information, an explanation of why the community in question was a good place for resettling refugees. The explanation had to do the following:

> Include an assessment of the availability of appropriate housing, public transportation, and employment opportunities. List other short- and long-term resettlement and integration services available at this site and in this community. If this site is able to serve special needs cases, describe what type of special needs cases it can serve and how it is able to do so. If the site expects to resettle refugee groups from nationalities /ethnicities new to the resettlement location, please provide an assessment of the site's capacity for resettling the anticipated new groups. [22]

The abstracts also had to include information about consultations the affiliates held:

> Describe the date, content, and result of consultative discussions undertaken by the affiliate with state and local officials and stakeholders in preparing this proposal, including the response of the state refugee coordinator and state refugee health coordinator. For new sites, include evidence of the above consultation and support of local affiliates, other service providers, and the state refugee coordinator of your plans.[23]

Decisions about which of the voluntary agencies will resettle particular approved refugee cases are made at weekly meetings at the Refugee Processing Center in Arlington, VA. According to the 2009 report *Refugee Crisis in America*, "these decisions are based on refugee biographical data ..., which includes information on family size, nationality, ethnicity, religion, and medical conditions."[24]

The voluntary agencies provide initial resettlement services using a combination of Reception and Placement Program funds and contributions from other sources. Until January 2010, the Reception and Placement grant per refugee was $900.

Effective January 1, 2010, DOS increased this per capita grant to $1,800. In announcing the increase, DOS stated: "The combined level of public and charitable resources available to the program is simply insufficient to do a quality job of initial resettlement." At least $1,100 of the $1,800 grant must be used for direct support of refugees; up to $700 may be used by the agencies for costs related to program management. [25]

Funding

Table 2 shows obligated funds[26] for the Reception and Placement Program, which increased throughout the period from FY2006 to FY2010. The increase in the per capita grant described above is reflected in the FY2010 total.

Table 2. Obligations for the Reception and Placement Program, FY2006-FY2010 (in millions)

Fiscal Year	Obligated Funds
FY2006	$49.9
FY2007	$56.9
FY2008	$67.9
FY2009	$90.0
FY2010	$141.9

Source: U.S. Department of State, Bureau of Population, Refugees, and Migration.
Notes: An obligation is a legal commitment to provide funding.

ORR Assistance

ORR benefits and services are available to refugees and other designated groups, as enumerated above. The refugee resettlement assistance program has been justified on the grounds that the admission of refugees to the United States is a decision of the federal government, entailing some federal responsibility. Unlike immigrants who enter through family or employment ties, refugees are admitted on humanitarian grounds and are not required to demonstrate economic self-support.

The INA sets forth four general requirements for the resettlement assistance program:

- "make available sufficient resources for employment training and placement in order to achieve economic self-sufficiency among refugees as quickly as possible;
- provide refugees with the opportunity to acquire sufficient English language training to enable them to become effectively resettled as quickly as possible;
- insure that cash assistance is made available to refugees in such a manner as not to discourage their economic self-sufficiency ... ; and
- ... insure that women have the same opportunities as men to participate in training and instruction."[27]

Types of Assistance

The INA authorizes the ORR director to provide for cash and medical assistance, social services projects, and targeted assistance for refugees.[28] These types of assistance are described in this section. The different ways in which this assistance is delivered to eligible refugees are described below.

Cash and Medical Assistance

According to ORR, refugees generally enter the United States without the necessary income or assets to support themselves during their first few months in the country. Those who meet the requirements for Temporary Assistance for Needy Families (TANF) or the Supplemental Security Income (SSI) program may receive assistance from these programs. Refugees are eligible for TANF for five years and SSI for seven years.[29] Refugees who meet the eligibility requirements for Medicaid may enroll in that program and receive Medicaid services for seven years.[30]

Some refugees meet the income and resource eligibility standards of these means-tested programs but are not categorically eligible for them. For example, single individuals and couples without children do not qualify for TANF. Historically, most nonelderly childless adults could not receive Medicaid.[31] Refugees who meet a program's financial requirements but are categorically ineligible for the program are eligible to receive special refugee cash assistance (RCA) and refugee medical assistance (RMA), as authorized by the INA.

Cash assistance under INA §412(e) for employable refugees is conditioned, with exceptions for good cause, on the refugee satisfying the following requirements:

- the refugee's registration with an appropriate agency or state or local employment service providing employment services;
- the refugee's participation in appropriate social service or targeted assistance programs providing job or language training; and
- the refugee's acceptance of appropriate job offers.

RCA and RMA are currently limited to a maximum of eight months.[32] The eligibility period begins at different points for different beneficiary groups. For example, individuals admitted as refugees who qualify for cash and medical assistance are eligible to receive these benefits during their first eight months in the United States. In the case of asylees, the eight-month eligibility period begins the month that the individual is granted asylum.

Social Services

INA §412(c) authorizes the refugee social services program. In accordance with the primary focus of the refugee assistance program on economic self-sufficiency, the ORR director is authorized to fund social services projects designed to

- "assist refugees in obtaining the skills which are necessary for economic self-sufficiency, including projects for job training, employment services, day care, professional refresher training, and other recertification services;
- provide training in English where necessary ... ; and
- provide, where specific needs have been shown and recognized by the Director, health (including mental health) services, social services, educational and other services."[33]

Social services funding is provided through formula grants to states and state-alternative programs (see description of Wilson-Fish authority, below) and through discretionary grants. Projects funded by formula grants are available to refugees who have been living in the United States for less than five years. By law, formula funding is allocated among the states based on the number of refugees who arrived in the United States not more than 36 months before the beginning of the fiscal year and who are living in the state as of the beginning of that year. In past years, these formula funds were allocated based on refugee arrivals in the last three years (the maximum allowable period). For FY2010, ORR revised the funding formula to base allocations on refugee arrivals in the last two years. According to ORR, "using only the most recent two-year arrival data will permit a more accurate allocation of funds based on the numbers and composition of the arriving populations."[34]

Social services discretionary grants are awarded in different program areas, as described below, to states, state-alternative programs, and nonprofit agencies. Discretionary grants may be used to provide services to refugees who have been in the United States for more than five years.

Targeted Assistance

Like social services funding, targeted assistance is intended to promote refugee employment and self-sufficiency. It benefits counties and similar areas in states where there is a demonstrated need for additional services for refugees "because of factors such as unusually large refugee populations (including secondary migration), high refugee concentrations, and high use of public assistance by refugees."[35]

Targeted assistance is provided through formula grants and discretionary grants. Ninety percent of targeted assistance funding is allocated by formula to states and state-alternative programs on behalf of eligible counties. In past years, these formula allocations were based on refugee arrivals during the prior five years. For FY2010, these allocations were based on arrivals data for the past two years. According to ORR, this formula change was required to meet the needs of newly arriving refugees. Meeting these refugees' needs soon after arrival, an ORR notice states, "is essential to ensuring their long-term self-sufficiency and integration."[36] With some exceptions, these formula funds cannot be used to provide services to refugees who have been in the United States for more than five years.

The remaining 10% of targeted assistance funding is awarded through competitive discretionary grants to states and state-alternative programs to implement special employment-related services. These services are not limited to refugees who have been living in the United States for less than five years.

Funding

Table 3 provides funding data for FY2006-FY2011 for selected ORR programs, including transitional and medical services (which includes cash and medical assistance),[37] social services, and targeted assistance.[38] Unlike Table 2, which shows obligated funds, Table 3 shows appropriations. For FY2011, the Administration is requesting funding increases for transitional and medical services and social services discretionary grants. The additional funding for transitional and medical services is being requested to establish a

$25 million contingency fund to ensure adequate program funding in the event of higher than expected costs due to economic conditions, refugee medical needs, or other factors.[39] The requested increase in social services funding would be used "to facilitate the path to self-sufficiency" during the recession by providing assistance to refugees facing emergencies, such as eviction and long-term unemployment.[40]

Table 3. Appropriations for Selected ORR Programs, FY2006-FY2011 (budget authority in millions)

Programs	FY2006 Actual	FY2007 Enacted	FY2008 Enacted	FY2009 Enacted	FY2010 Estimate	FY2011 Request
Transitional and	$265.4	$265.5	$296.1	$282.3	$353.3	$417.0
Medical Services						
Social Services	153.9	154.0	154.0	154.0	154.0	179.0
Targeted	48.6	48.6	48.6	48.6	48.6	48.6

Sources: U.S. Department of Health and Human Services, Administration for Children and Families, *Justifications of Estimates for Appropriations Committees*, FY2008-FY2011.

Approaches to Providing Assistance

Refugees in the United States may receive cash assistance, medical assistance, and employment-related services through different types of programs depending on where they live and what their particular circumstances are. Refugees may receive resettlement assistance through a state-administered program, a Public/Private Partnership program, a Voluntary Agency Matching Grant Program, and/or a Wilson/Fish program.

State-Administered Program

Most eligible refugees receive resettlement assistance through a state-administered program. ORR reimburses states for the full costs of their refugee cash assistance and refugee medical assistance programs. State-administered RCA payments to eligible refugees are based on the state/county TANF payment to a family unit of the same size and RMA benefits are based on the state's Medicaid program.[41] States may opt to have state-administered programs if they "believe the public delivery system has the expertise required to provide services more effectively and efficiently than community-based organizations."[42]

For FY2010, states with state-administered programs received formula social services grants based on the number of refugee arrivals in the last two years who were living in the state as of the beginning of the fiscal year, as explained above. States may also receive competitively awarded social services discretionary grants in five program areas: Cuban/Haitian; Preventive Health; School Impact; Services to Older Refugees; and Targeted Assistance. (A separate set of social services discretionary grants for public and private, nonprofit agencies is discussed below.)

With respect to targeted assistance, as discussed above, states receive formula grants on behalf of eligible counties. States may also receive competitive discretionary grants to implement special employment-related services.

Public/Private Partnership

Under HHS/ORR regulations, states have the option of establishing an RCA program that is a "public/private partnership" (PPP) between the state and local resettlement agencies, or maintaining a publicly administered RCA program.[43] The local resettlement agencies are the local affiliates of the voluntary agencies that provide initial resettlement services under the Reception and Placement Program. States may choose to establish a PPP program in order "to strengthen the link between the initial placement of refugees and the RCA and social service programs, providing services more seamlessly."[44]

Payment levels under a public/private RCA program may be higher than under a state-administered program.[45] PPP programs currently operate in five states: Maryland, Minnesota, Oklahoma, Oregon, and Texas. The public/private partnership model does not include the RMA program. That program continues to be state-administered.

Wilson/Fish Authority

The "Wilson/Fish amendment," enacted as part of the FY1985 Continuing Appropriations Resolution,[46] added language to the INA directing the HHS Secretary to develop alternatives to state-administered refugee resettlement assistance. Under these alternative Wilson/Fish projects, refugees are to be provided with "interim support, medical services, support services, and case management, as needed, in a manner that encourages self-sufficiency, reduces welfare dependency, and fosters greater coordination among the resettlement agencies and service providers."[47]

Another purpose of the Wilson/Fish program is to ensure that there are refugee assistance programs in all states where refugees are resettled.[48] Thus, ORR funds Wilson/Fish projects that establish or maintain a refugee program in a state that either is not participating in the refugee program or is withdrawing from the program, in whole or in part. (These are examples of state-alternative programs, as referenced above.)[49]

ORR currently funds Wilson/Fish programs in 12 states (Alabama, Alaska, Colorado, Idaho, Kentucky, Louisiana, Massachusetts, Nevada, North Dakota, South Dakota, Tennessee, Vermont) and one county (San Diego County, CA). Funds for Wilson/Fish projects are drawn from refugee cash and medical assistance funds and social services formula allocations. Wilson/Fish projects also may receive competitively awarded social services grants and targeted assistance grants.

According to ORR, common elements of Wilson/Fish alternative projects include the following:

- "creation of a 'front-loaded' service system which provides intensive services to refugees in the early months after arrival with an emphasis on early employment;
- integration of case management, cash assistance, and employment services generally under a single agency that is culturally and linguistically equipped to work with refugees; and
- innovative strategies for the provision of cash assistance, through incentives, bonuses and income disregards which are tied directly to the achievement of employment goals outlined in the client self-sufficiency plan."[50]

Wilson/Fish projects may provide the same higher payment levels as PPP programs[51] (discussed above) and may provide cash assistance to TANF-eligible refugees. ORR's new Wilson/Fish announcement, however, sets forth a set of requirements that must be met in order for Wilson/ Fish cash and medical assistance funds to be provided to TANF-eligible refugees.[52]

Voluntary Agency Matching Grant Program

The Voluntary Agency Matching Grant (MG) Program is an alternative to traditional state-administered RCA programs and other public cash assistance. Under the MG Program, voluntary resettlement agencies assume responsibility for resettling refugees and helping them become self-sufficient within their first four or six months in the United States. These voluntary agencies are the same agencies that have cooperative agreements with DOS under the Reception and Placement Program. Services provided to refugees through the MG program include case management, job placement and follow up, interim housing, and interim cash assistance.

There are MG program sites in most states. According to ORR, in calendar year 2009 there were 233 sites in 45 states.[53] Under the MG Program, voluntary agencies provide a one dollar match (in cash and/or in-kind services) for every two federal dollars. Federal funding for the program is drawn from transitional and medical services funds. Each year, the ORR director decides how much funding to allot to the MG program.

The MG program is voluntary for both the refugee and the voluntary agency. In order for a refugee case to be eligible for the MG program, at least one person in the refugee unit must be deemed to be employable. Refugees who are eligible for their state's TANF program can be enrolled in the MG program. While participating in the MG program, however, refugees may not receive TANF, RCA, or other public cash assistance, or employability services funded by formula social services or targeted assistance grants. They may receive RMA.[54]

Discretionary Social Services Grants to Public and Private, Nonprofit Agencies

As discussed above, ORR provides competitive social services discretionary grants and targeted assistance discretionary grants to states. ORR also competitively awards social services discretionary funds to public agencies and nonprofit organizations in eight program areas: Preferred Communities, Services for Unanticipated Arrivals, Ethnic Community Self-Help Organizations, Microenterprise Development, Individual Development Accounts, Technical Assistance, Refugee Agriculture Partnership, and Healthy Marriage.[55]

Choice of Approaches

States use different combinations of the approaches described above to deliver resettlement assistance. A 2008 evaluation of the refugee social services and targeted assistance programs that synthesized findings from sites in California, Florida, and Texas included a discussion of the different ways in which RCA and social services were provided in the three states. In the case of Texas, for example, the report explained that the state provided refugee cash assistance to individuals who were not eligible for TANF through a public/private partnership arrangement. In addition, through the Matching

Grant program, voluntary agencies in Texas provided cash benefits to TANF-eligible families that were greater than the equivalent TANF benefits. The report offered the following explanation for this approach:

> In Texas, the state offers one of the lowest TANF benefits in the country. In addition, the state receives a highly diverse and continually changing group of refugees each year, requiring a level of cultural competency that the Volags [voluntary agencies] can provide but the state lacks. By using a PPP, in combination with reserving Matching Grant funds for families, the state is able to provide greater benefits for a limited time and use organizations familiar with the refugee population to provide services.

By contrast, Florida has a state-administered refugee assistance program. The report noted that, unlike Texas, Florida receives a relatively stable group of refugees from Cuba and Haiti. According to the report, "over time, the welfare and other service agencies have developed the cultural understanding required to serve this population."[56]

CURRENT ISSUES IN REFUGEE RESETTLEMENT ASSISTANCE

In recent years, as noted above, the United States has admitted an increasingly diverse group of refugees. In its FY2011 budget request for ORR, the Obama Administration highlighted some of the needs of today's refugees:

> Changing demographics of the U.S. resettlement program present new challenges, as many populations require extended employment services to gain a toehold in the U.S. labor market and integrate into U.S. society. Many recent arrivals have spent protracted amounts of time in refugee camps in countries of first asylum, have experienced intense trauma and have disabilities. Many arriving refugees have limited work skills, cannot read and write in their own language and require intensive English as a Second Language (ESL) courses prior to employment.[57]

The recent experiences of arriving refugees and resettlement communities have raised many questions about the adequacy of the existing refugee resettlement assistance program to meet the needs of refugees and help them successfully integrate into American society. A 2010 congressional report by minority staff of the Senate Foreign Relations Committee concluded that the current systems of refugee admissions and resettlement "are out-dated and fail to address the needs of the culturally and linguistically diverse populations now being admitted to the United States." The report, based on field research conducted in Indiana and Georgia, also chronicled the strains the current system places on local communities.[58] A May 2010 report by the Columbia University School of International and Public Affairs (SIPA) on the U.S. refugee admissions and resettlement programs determined that:

> increasing demographic diversity among the arriving refugee population and a shifting focus toward resettling the most vulnerable has tested the limits of the U.S. resettlement system and has revealed serious problem areas.[59]

Several other recent reports have focused on the resettlement of Iraqi refugees in the United States.[60] For example, in June 2009 the International Rescue Committee (IRC), one of the voluntary agencies that helps resettle refugees in the United States, published a report based on the experiences of Iraqi refugees resettled in Atlanta, GA, and Phoenix, AZ.[61] The above-cited *Refugee Crisis in America* focused on Iraqi refugees resettled in Detroit, MI; San Diego, CA; and Washington, DC. While highlighting particular challenges faced by newly arriving Iraqi refugees, these reports also raised larger questions about the resettlement assistance program.

Broad Challenges

The U.S. refugee resettlement assistance program faces a number of broad challenges, several of which are described here.

Interagency Coordination and Information Sharing

As discussed above, DOS's PRM and HHS's ORR both administer refugee resettlement assistance programs. The Columbia University SIPA report quoted the Assistant Secretary of State for PRM as writing in 2010 that, during site visits, he "observed weak linkages between the State Department's initial Reception and Placement Program and the longer-term services to refugees provided by the Department of Health and Human Services."[62]

More generally, several reports have noted the lack of information collection and sharing by and among the many agencies and organizations involved in the U.S. refugee admissions and resettlement systems. "In some cases," according to *Refugee Crisis in America*, "information is gathered [in overseas processing] that is not shared with agencies further down the resettlement chain, increasing the likelihood that refugee needs will not be met."[63] Along the same lines, the SIPA report referred to "gaps in information sharing" between federal and local agencies in the refugee placement decision-making process, and limited information sharing about refugee cases between PRM and organizations that conduct overseas refugee processing on the one hand and the voluntary agencies in the Reception and Placement Program on the other.[64]

Funding

Recent reports, such as the above-cited IRC report and *Refugee Crisis in America*, have concluded that federal funding for resettlement assistance is inadequate to enable refugees to achieve long-term sufficiency and integration. These reports variously found that insufficient funding is provided for cash assistance, employment services, English language training, education, housing, and medical treatment, among other services.

The allocation formulas for social services and targeted assistance funding are another issue. As discussed above, prior to FY2010 social services formula funds were allocated based on refugee arrivals in the last three years and targeted assistance formula funds were allocated based on refugee arrivals in the last five years. While these formulas were revised in FY2010 to base allocations on refugee arrivals in the past two years, some observers argue that even a two-year period is too long and negatively impacts the ability of service providers to meet the needs of refugees, especially in locations with new surging refugee populations.

Resettlement Communities and Secondary Migration

The July 2010 report by the Senate Foreign Relations Committee minority staff discussed the strain the refugee resettlement system places on local communities. It noted that local governments do not have a formal role in the process of deciding where to resettle refugees and "often are not even informed in advance that new residents will be arriving."[65] The report indicated that resettlement communities are not provided with either information about the educational, health, or other needs of incoming refugees, or sufficient resources to address these needs. [66] As noted above, funding for social services and targeted assistance is based on past refugee admissions. Observers have maintained that this system leaves newer resettlement communities without needed resources to serve these new arrivals.

Secondary migration can pose significant challenges for some communities and for the migrants themselves. Refugees who are initially resettled in a particular area are free to move anywhere else in the United States that they choose. According to *Refugee Crisis in America*, "there are no adequate mechanisms in place for anticipating foreseeable trends in secondary migration." The report further states that the failure to track secondary migration while it is occurring prevents resources from being directed to areas of need. Under the existing system, when refugees relocate to new communities, "resettlement assistance often lags behind or becomes difficult to access."[67]

Self-Sufficiency Model

More fundamentally, some observers question whether the historical approach to refugee resettlement, with an across-the-board emphasis on quick employment, is appropriate or effective.

Refugee Crisis in America described this approach, implemented through mainstream public assistance programs such as TANF and Medicaid, as "misguided." According to the report:

> Refugees who have fled persecution in foreign countries face an utterly different set of challenges than do U.S. residents struggling with poverty. In addition to struggling with poverty themselves, refugees must rebuild their lives in a foreign country, learn a new language and adapt to a new way of life.[68]

The 2009 IRC report on Iraqi refugees identified the particular barriers this population faces in resettling in the United States, including high levels of trauma and illness. The report further described the difficulties faced by the many Iraqi widows with young children who lack employment experience but are nevertheless expected to quickly find employment to support their families.

Key Issues in Resettlement Assistance

The broad challenges outlined above provide context for a host of particular concerns about the resettlement assistance program. Some key issues are highlighted here.

Financial Assistance to Refugees

As described above, needy refugees can generally receive Refugee Cash Assistance for up to eight months or can receive public cash assistance through the TANF program. Some observers argue that eight months of cash assistance is insufficient to enable refugees to become self-supporting, especially during the current economic situation. In the past, as noted above, RCA was available for a longer period, but as appropriations levels decreased over the years, the coverage period was reduced to the current eight months.

The dollar amount of cash assistance provided to refugees is similarly criticized by some as being insufficient. According to the 2009 International Rescue Committee report, assistance received by refugees is "often insufficient to cover the cost of rent and basic necessities." The report also indicated that many refugees interviewed said that "their relatives in Iraq are sending them money to help cover basic needs such as housing."[69]

"Lottery" Effect

The levels of cash assistance received by most refugees, whether through the RCA program or TANF, are based on TANF rates for a family of the relevant size. These rates vary by state and county. As a result of this "lottery" system, refugees resettled in different parts of the United States may receive very different levels of assistance. "Inevitably," according to a 2010 report by Columbia University's School of International and Public Affairs, "those individuals and families who are fortunate enough to be resettled in states with generous social welfare programs end up better off than those in states that offer less assistance."[70]

Communities in which refugees are resettled and voluntary agencies to which refugee cases are assigned also differ in ways that may significantly affect the ability of a refugee to successfully resettle in the United States. For example, communities may differ in their public transportation systems and in their attitudes toward and willingness to offer support to new refugees. Voluntary agencies may differ in the specialized services they provide, among other ways.[71]

Emphasis on Quick Employment

The U.S. refugee resettlement program is predicated on the idea that newly arriving refugees can and should find employment within a relatively short period of time. Obtaining employment has been particularly difficult, however, in the current economic climate. The FY2011 budget justification for ORR discusses economic challenges facing incoming refugees. It provides an example of refugees from Burma, Bhutan, and Burundi who lack work experience, education, and English proficiency and have "very few skills that translate to the U.S. labor market."[72]

Refugees who were professionals in their home countries face their own set of challenges. They are often unable to find comparable jobs in the United States. Recent reports about Iraqi refugees have discussed the effect of the refugee program's emphasis on employment on Iraqi professionals and the caseworkers who assist in their resettlement.

The 2009 IRC report described the experience of educated Iraqis who had been established in their professions in Iraq:

> As refugees begin to grasp the reality of the job market and the cost of living in America, they realize they need to accept any job as soon as possible, even if it does not make full use of their professional background. Many Iraqis pointed out that their potential is being wasted and that they could make greater contributions to American society if they were given sufficient time and resources to recertify in their professions.[73]

Refugee Crisis in America reported that caseworkers "push Iraqi refugees towards lower-paying and less sustainable jobs" regardless of their professional and educational credentials. It further argued that "the limited duration of public assistance makes pursuing recertification, vocational training, and higher education untenable without financial aid from the government."[74]

Health Care Needs of Refugees

Increasing numbers of incoming refugees have serious health conditions. According to the FY2011 budget justifications for ORR:

> The number of refugees with chronic untreated medical and mental health conditions continues to grow as the number of refugees coming to the United States who have lived their entire lives in inadequate refugee camp settings with limited access to medical care and nutrition grows. These health problems must be treated before the refugees can enter employment.[75]

As explained above, needy refugees who do not qualify for Medicaid are limited to up to eight months of RMA.

The poor physical and mental health of incoming Iraqi refugees has been discussed in recent reports on this population. According to the IRC report,

Iraqi refugees have "higher degrees of emotional trauma" and are "in poorer shape overall" than other refugee groups.[76]

English Language Instruction

Proficiency in the English language is widely seen as a key factor in achieving economic self-sufficiency. Refugee caseworkers have identified lack of English language ability as the main reason that Iraqi refugees cannot find long-term employment.[77] Lack of English language ability can also make it difficult for refugees to access health care and communicate with law enforcement officers, with potential consequences for both general public health and safety.

Although the INA directs ORR, in providing resettlement assistance, to give refugees "the opportunity to acquire sufficient English language training,"[78] recent reports indicate that quality instruction is not available widely enough. According to *Refugee Crisis in America*, "refugees have difficulty accessing English language training, the quality of instruction is poor, and there are simply not enough classes available for all refugees."[79]

Potential Policy Options

The above discussion of challenges and issues facing the refugee resettlement assistance program suggests many potential areas for reform. It also suggests that policy changes could be pursued within the basic framework of the existing system or that the system itself could be redesigned. Some changes could be made within existing law, while others would require legislative action. The selected options presented here, which have been drawn from a variety of sources, are grouped into two main substantive categories—administration and planning, and ORR programs—although there is overlap both between options included in a single category and between categories.

Administration and Planning

Policy options in this category concern the overall administration of resettlement assistance and the interactions between the various agencies and other entities that have a role in the resettlement system.

Coordination of the U.S. Refugee Program

One agency could be given responsibility for coordinating all the entities involved in refugee admissions and resettlement.[80] This lead agency could then establish policies and procedures to ensure consistency and continuity as refugees are admitted and resettled in the United States.

Information Sharing

Information-sharing mechanisms could be instituted among the agencies and organizations involved in the refugee program. For example, information collected by organizations that conduct overseas processing could be systematically shared with ORR, voluntary agencies, and local affiliates in the United States to enable them to anticipate the needs of new arrivals. PRM and ORR could also improve communication and information sharing about refugee cases.

Placement and Receiving Communities

Another set of options to reform the refugee resettlement system concerns resettlement communities. State and local officials could be given a formal role in the refugee placement process. Information-sharing mechanisms could also be established among voluntary agencies on the one hand and local officials and service providers in receiving communities on the other. This information sharing could be two-way, with local communities providing information about their capacities to aid in the placement decision-making process and voluntary agencies providing information about the needs of arriving populations.

Secondary Migration

A mechanism could be established to track secondary migration in real time. This information could then be used to determine where additional resettlement resources were needed. In addition, the formulas for allocating social services and targeted assistance funding could be revised to make them more responsive to unplanned arrivals. Another related reform option would be to establish a system to make it easier for refugees who relocate to receive Reception and Placement Program and ORR assistance in their new communities.

ORR Programs

These options concern ORR's refugee resettlement assistance programs, which include cash assistance, medical assistance, and social services. Options under the funding category are limited to funding increases. Options under the other categories would involve broader changes to existing ORR programs, although they also may require additional funding.

Funding

Many observers have recommended an increase in funding for existing programs, such as cash assistance and social services. Additional funding could be provided to increase monthly refugee cash assistance benefits and/or extend the current eight-month maximum eligibility period. Additional funding could also be used to expand the Voluntary Agency Matching Grant Program, which is considered by many to be more effective than traditional state-administered cash assistance. Increased funding could also be targeted to particular employment-related services, such as English language training.

Mental Health Services

Recent reports on Iraqi refugees have argued that refugees do not have access to adequate medical care, including treatment for serious mental health conditions. One of many possible options related to health care would be to expand mental health services—both traditional and nontraditional—to address the needs of refugees who have experienced torture or severe trauma.

Restructuring Cash Assistance

As indicated above, many observers have argued that refugee cash assistance levels are inadequate and should be increased. Another broader reform option would be to de-link refugee cash assistance from TANF and make payment levels uniform across the United States. These nationwide cash assistance levels could be set at the payment levels under a public/private refugee cash assistance program, as set forth in HHS regulations (see above), or at another level.

Restructuring Employment Services

The across-the-board focus on quick employment and economic self-sufficiency could be modified to tailor employment services to the particular needs and backgrounds of incoming refugees in order to improve their long-term employment prospects. For example, job recertification and job placement programs could be made available to refugees with professional backgrounds. Vocational training could be made available to certain refugees to teach them marketable job skills.

CONCLUSION

The circumstances and needs of newly arriving refugees, coupled with the economic downturn, have focused attention on the refugee resettlement assistance issue. The Obama Administration has taken steps to provide additional resources for selected assistance programs. Many observers believe, however, that more far-reaching reform of the resettlement assistance system is necessary to enable refugees to achieve successful resettlement and integration. It remains unclear whether the Administration will take additional steps to reform the system and/or whether Congress will pursue reform through legislation. It may be that the results of the NSC-led interagency review mentioned in the introduction will help galvanize support for a particular set of reforms.

End Notes

[1] U.S. Department of State, U.S. Department of Homeland Security, and U.S. Department of Health and Human Services, *Proposed Refugee Admissions for Fiscal Year 2011: Report to the Congress*, pp. ii-iii.

[2] Anna Gorman and Alexandra Zavis, "U.S. Wants to Make it Easier for Refugees; Obama officals will review a System They Say is Outdated and lacks the resources to Help New Arrivals Get on Their Feet," *Los Angeles Times*, June 23, 2010, p. A12.

[3] INA is act of June 27, 1952, ch. 477, codified, as amended, at 8 U.S.C. §§ 1101 *et seq.* The Refugee Act is P.L. 96- 212, March 17, 1980.

[4] The other components of permanent admissions are family-based immigrants, employment-based immigrants, and diversity immigrants. See CRS Report RL32235, *U.S. Immigration Policy on Permanent Admissions*, by Ruth Ellen Wasem.

[5] INA §207. For further discussion of the refugee admissions process, see CRS Report RL31269, *Refugee Admissions and Resettlement Policy*, by Andorra Bruno.

[6] INA §101(a)(42).

[7] INA §208.

[8] P.L. 96-422, §501(e), October 10, 1980, as amended, 8 U.S.C. §1522 note. See CRS Report RS21349, *U.S. Immigration Policy on Haitian Migrants*, by Ruth Ellen Wasem. Eligibility for refugee benefits is provided for in P.L. 96-422, §501(e).

[9] P.L. 106-386, §107(b)(1)(C), October 28, 2000. A severe form of trafficking is defined in §103(8) of the act. See CRS Report RL34317, *Trafficking in Persons: U.S. Policy and Issues for Congress*, by Alison Siskin and Liana Sun Wyler.

[10] §584(b) of P.L. 100-202, §101(e), December 22, 1987, as amended, 8 U.S.C. §1101 note.

[11] P.L. 109-163, Div. A, Title X, §1059, January 6, 2006, as amended, 8 U.S.C. §1522 note.

[12] P.L. 110-181, Div. A, Title XII, §1244, January 28, 2008, as amended, 8 U.S.C. §1157 note. Section 1244(c), as amended, places a numerical limitation of 5,000 per year for FY2008-FY2012 on principal aliens who may be granted special immigrant status under the program.

[13] P.L. 111-8, Division F, Title VI, §602, March 11, 2009, as amended. Section §602(b)(3) places a numerical limitation of 1,500 per year for FY2009-FY2013 on principal aliens who may be granted special immigrant status under the program.

[14] U.S. Department of Justice, Immigration and Naturalization Service, *1986 Statistical Yearbook of the Immigration and Naturalization Service*, Table 23 ("Refugee Arrivals into the United States by Selected Nationality, Fiscal Years 1982-86"), p. 42.

[15] Georgetown Human Rights Action and Georgetown University Law Center, Human Rights Institute, *Refugee Crisis in America: Iraqis and Their Resettlement Experience*, 2009, pp. 25-26, http://www.law.georgetown.edu/news/releases/documents/RefugeeCrisisinAmerica_000.pdf (hereafter cited as *Refugee Crisis in America*).

[16] See CRS Report RL33809, Noncitizen Eligibility for Federal Public Assistance: Policy Overview and Trends, by Ruth Ellen Wasem.

[17] INA §412.

[18] Information on services for refugee minors, unaccompanied alien children, and survivors of torture is available on the ORR website, http://www.acf.hhs.gov/programs/orr/programs/index.htm. As noted above, victims of trafficking are eligible for ORR programs for refugees. ORR also funds separate programs for victims of trafficking; see CRS Report RL34317, *Trafficking in Persons: U.S. Policy and Issues for Congress*, by Alison Siskin and Liana Sun Wyler.

[19] U.S. President (Carter), "Letter to the Speaker of the House and the President of the Senate Transmitting a Study. January 13, 1981," *Weekly Compilation of Presidential Documents*, vol. 17 (January 20, 1981), p. 2880.

[20] At present, the voluntary agencies are Church World Service (CWS); Ethiopian Community Development Council (ECDC); Episcopal Migration Ministries (EMM); Hebrew Immigrant Aid Society (HIAS); International Rescue Committee (IRC); Kurdish Human Rights Watch, Inc. (KHRW); Lutheran Immigration and Refugee Services (LIRS); U.S. Committee for Refugees and Immigrants (USCRI); U.S. Conference of Catholic Bishops (USCCB); World Relief Corporation (WR); and State of Iowa, Bureau of Refugee Services. Links to these agencies' websites are available at
http://www.acf.hhs.gov/programs/orr/partners/voluntary_agencies

[21] 8 U.S.C. §1522(a)(2)(A).

[22] U.S. Department of State, Bureau of Population, Refugees, and Migration, *FY2011 Funding Opportunity Announcement for Reception and Placement Program*, May 12, 2010, http://www.state

[23] Ibid.

[24] Refugee Crisis in America, p. 9.

[25] U.S. Department of State, "Increase to the Refugee Reception and Placement Per Capita Grant," press release, January 25, 2010.

[26] An obligation is a legal commitment to provide funding. Separate appropriations data are not available for the Reception and Placement Program. This program is included in the larger DOS appropriation for Migration & Refugee Assistance.

[27] INA §412(a)(1)(A).

[28] INA §§412(c), (e).

[29] A temporary provision (in P.L. 110-328, September 30, 2008) extends to nine years (during FY2009 through FY2011) the period of eligibility of certain refugees and others for SSI benefits, provided that specified criteria are met.

[30] After the eligibility periods for TANF (of five years) and Medicaid (of seven years), refugees may continue to receive services from these programs at state option. For further information, see CRS Report RL33809, *Noncitizen Eligibility for Federal Public Assistance: Policy Overview and Trends*, by Ruth Ellen Wasem.

[31] Recent changes to the Medicaid statute in the Patient Protection and Affordable Care Act (PPACA; P.L. 111-148) have expanded coverage. Among the changes, beginning in 2014 (or sooner at state option), states must provide Medicaid coverage to all nonelderly, childless adults whose income falls below a specified threshold and who do not qualify under another mandatory category. See CRS Report RL33202, *Medicaid: A Primer*, by Elicia J. Herz.

[32] INA §412(e)(1) authorizes ORR to reimburse states for RCA and RMA for 36 months. Initially, beginning in April 1980, RCA and RMA were available for the full 36 months. As appropriations levels decreased in subsequent years, however, the period of coverage was reduced. Since October 1991, RCA and RMA have been available for eight months.

[33] INA §412(c)(1)(A).

[34] Department of Health and Human Services, Administration for Children and Families, Office of Refugee Resettlement, *Notice of Final FY 2010 Formula Allocations to States for Refugee Social Services*, HHS-2010-ACF-ORR-ORRRS-0119, p. 8, available at http://www.acf.hhs.gov/grants

[35] INA §412(c)(2)(A).

[36] Department of Health and Human Services, Administration for Children and Families, Office of Refugee Resettlement, *Notice of Final FY 2010 Formula Allocations to States for Targeted Assistance Grants to States for Services to Refugees*, HHS-2010-ACF-ORR-ORRTA-0118, p. 7, available at http://www.acf.hhs.gov/grants

[37] In addition to cash and medical assistance, transitional and medical services includes funding for unaccompanied refugee minors and minors who are victims of trafficking.

[38] For funding data on other ORR programs, see CRS Report RL31269, *Refugee Admissions and Resettlement Policy*, by Andorra Bruno.

[39] U.S. Department of Health and Human Services, Administration for Children and Families, *Justifications of Estimates for Appropriations Committees*, FY2011, p. 228 (hereafter cited as ACF/ORR budget justifications for FY2011).

[40] Ibid., pp. 241-242.

[41] ORR does not reimburse states for their costs for the TANF, SSI, and Medicaid programs.

[42] Mary Farrel, Bret Barden, and Mike Mueller, The Evaluation of the Refugee Social Service (RSS) and Targeted Assistance Formula Grant (TAG) Programs: Synthesis of Findings from Three Sites, prepared for U.S. Department of Health and Human Services, Office of Refugee Resettlement, by The Lewin Group, March 2008, p. 16 (hereafter cited as The Evaluation of the Refugee Social Service (RSS) and Targeted Assistance Formula Grant (TAG) Programs).

[43] The underlying final rule was published in 2000. See U.S. Department of Health and Human Services, Office of Refugee Resettlement, "Refugee Resettlement Program; Requirements for Refugee Cash Assistance; and Refugee Medical Assistance," 65 *Federal Register*, March 22, 2000, pp. 15409-15450.

[44] The Evaluation of the Refugee Social Service (RSS) and Targeted Assistance Formula Grant (TAG) Programs, p. 16.

[45] Monthly payment ceilings under a public/private RCA program, by size of the family unit, are set forth in 45 C.F.R. §400.60. Payments under a public/private RCA program, however, may not be lower than the state's TANF payment level for a same-sized family unit.

[46] P.L. 98-473, Title I, §101(d), October 12, 1984.

[47] INA §412(e)(7)(A). Wilson/Fish projects that provide alternative approaches for delivering refugee assistance and services are sometimes referred to as Category II projects.

[48] All states except Wyoming have a refugee assistance program.

[49] State-alternative Wilson/Fish projects are sometimes referred to as Category I projects.

[50] ORR FY2007 annual report, p. 16.

[51] According to ORR, although Wilson/Fish projects are not required to provide the higher payment rates (in 45 C.F.R. 444.60), most projects do. E-mail from ORR to CRS, September 29, 2010.

[52] Among these requirements, the state TANF rate must be lower than the maximum allowable Wilson/Fish payment level and the state must provide the full amount of the TANF rate to the refugee. Subject to the availability of appropriated funds, if all applicable criteria are met Wilson/Fish funds could be used to provide a differential payment to cover the difference between the state TANF rate and the Wilson/Fish payment level. See Department of Health and Human Services, Administration for Children and Families, Office of Refugee Resettlement, *Wilson/Fish Alternative Program*, HHS-2010-ACF-ORR-RW-0051, p. 4-5, available at http://www.acf.hhs.gov/grants

[53] A list of these sites is available on the ORR website at http://www.acf.hhs.gov/programs/orr/programs/mgpss.htm.

[54] The matching grant program dates back to 1979. For historical information about the program, see http://www.acf.hhs.gov/programs/orr/programs/index.htm.

[55] Information about these programs is available on the ORR website at http://www.acf.hhs.gov/programs/orr/.

[56] The Evaluation of the Refugee Social Service (RSS) and Targeted Assistance Formula Grant (TAG) Programs, pp. 15-16.

[57] ACF/ORR budget justifications for FY2011.

[58] U.S. Congress, Senate Foreign Relations Committee, Abandoned Upon Arrival: Implications for Refugees and Local Communities Burdened by a U.S. Resettlement System That Is Not Working, committee print, 111th Cong., 2nd sess., July 21, 2010 (Washington, DC: GPO, 2010) (hereafter cited as Abandoned Upon Arrival).

[59] Columbia University School of International and Public Affairs, *Refugee Resettlement in the United States: An Examination of Challenges and Proposed Solutions*, May 2010, pp. 14-15, (hereafter cited as Columbia University SIPA report).

[60] According to PRM data, a total of 18,016 Iraqi refugees were resettled in the United States in FY2009, more than from any other country.

[61] International Rescue Committee, *Iraqi Refugees in the United States: In Dire Straits*, June 2009, http://www.theirc.org/sites/default/files/resource-file/irc_report_iraqcommission.pdf (hereafter cited as IRC report).

[62] Columbia University SIPA report, p. 17.

[63] Refugee Crisis in America, p. 36.

[64] Columbia University SIPA report, pp. 11-12.

[65] Abandoned Upon Arrival, p. 2.

[66] Ibid., pp. vi, 3.

[67] Refugee Crisis in America, p. 35.

[68] Ibid., p. 26.

[69] IRC report, p. 7.

[70] Columbia University SIPA report, pp. 14-15, citing other sources.

[71] See Ibid., pp. 14-15, citing other sources.

[72] ACF/ORR budget justifications for FY2011, p. 241.

[73] IRC report, p. 8.

[74] Refugee Crisis in America, p. 25.

[75] ACF/ORR budget justifications for FY2011, p. 228.

[76] IRC report, p. 9.

[77] Refugee Crisis in America, p. 22.

[78] INA §412(a)(1)(A).

[79] Refugee Crisis in America, p. 22.

[80] For example, the authors of *Refugee Crisis in America* recommend that the White House identify a lead agency to coordinate all agencies and organizations in the refugee program; *Refugee Crisis in America*, p. 43.

In: Refugee Resettlement in the United States ISBN: 978-1-62257-962-4
Editors: R. J. Irvin and L. Gambrell

Chapter 3

REFUGEE RESETTLEMENT: GREATER CONSULTATION WITH COMMUNITY STAKEHOLDERS COULD STRENGTHEN PROGRAM*

United States Government Accountability Office

WHY GAO DID THIS STUDY

In fiscal year 2011, the United States admitted more than 56,000 refugees under its refugee resettlement program. Upon entry, a network of private, nonprofit voluntary agencies (voluntary agencies) selects the communities where refugees will live. The Department of State's PRM and the Department of Health and Human Services' ORR provide funding to help refugees settle in their communities and obtain employment and monitor implementation of the program. Congress has begun to reexamine the refugee resettlement program, and GAO was asked to examine (1) the factors resettlement agencies consider when determining where refugees are initially placed; (2) the effects refugees have on their communities; (3) how federal agencies ensure program effectiveness and integrity; and (4) what is known about the integration of refugees. GAO reviewed agency guidance, monitoring protocols, reports, and

---

* This is an edited, reformatted and augmented version of United States Government Accountability Office, Publication No. GAO-12-729, dated July 2012.

studies; conducted a literature review; reviewed and analyzed relevant federal and state laws and regulations; and met with federal and state officials, voluntary agency staff, and local stakeholders in eight selected communities.

WHAT GAO RECOMMENDS

GAO makes several recommendations to the Secretaries of State and Health and Human Services to improve refugee assistance programs in the United States. HHS and State generally concurred with the recommendations and each identified efforts they have under way or plan to undertake to address them.

WHAT GAO FOUND

Voluntary agencies consider various factors when determining where refugees will be placed, but few agencies we visited consulted relevant local stakeholders, which posed challenges for service providers. When deciding how many refugees to place in each community, some voluntary agencies prioritize local agency capacity, such as staffing levels, while others emphasize community capacity, such as housing availability. Although the Immigration and Nationality Act states that it is the intent of Congress for voluntary agencies to work closely with state and local stakeholders when making these decisions, the Department of State's Bureau of Population, Refugees, and Migration (PRM) offers limited guidance on how this should occur. Some communities GAO visited had developed formal processes for obtaining stakeholder input after receiving an overwhelming number of refugees, but most had not, which made it difficult for health care providers and school systems to prepare for and properly serve refugees.

State and local stakeholders reported that refugees bring cultural diversity and stimulate economic development, but serving refugees can stretch local resources, including safety net services. In addition, refugee students can negatively affect performance outcomes for school districts because they often have limited English proficiency. Furthermore, some refugees choose to relocate after their initial placement, and this secondary migration may stretch communities that do not have adequate resources to serve them. In fact, capacity challenges have led some communities to request restrictions or temporary moratoriums on resettlement.

PRM and the Department of Health and Human Services' Office of Refugee Resettlement (ORR) monitor their refugee assistance programs, but weaknesses in performance measurement may hinder effectiveness. Although refugees are eligible for ORR services for up to 5 years, the outcome data that ORR collects focuses on shorter-term employment outcomes. ORR officials said that their performance measurement reflects the goals outlined by the Immigration and Nationality Act—to help refugees achieve economic self-sufficiency as quickly as possible. However, the focus on rapid employment makes it difficult to provide services that may increase refugees' incomes, such as helping them obtain credentials to practice their professions in the United States.

Little is known about the extent of refugee integration into U.S. communities, but research offers a framework for measuring and facilitating integration. PRM and ORR both promote refugee integration, but neither agency currently measures integration as a program outcome. While integration is part of ORR's mission, ORR officials said one of the reasons they have not measured it is that there is no clear definition of integration. In addition, research on refugee resettlement does not offer an overall assessment of how well refugees have integrated into the United States. Most of the 13 studies GAO reviewed were limited in scope and focused on particular refugee groups in specific geographic locations. However, these studies identified a variety of indicators that can be used to assess integration as well as factors that can facilitate integration, such as English language acquisition, employment, and social support from other refugees. Despite limited national information, some U.S. communities have developed formal plans for refugee integration.

ABBREVIATIONS

DHS	Department of Homeland Security
HHS	Department of Health and Human Services
ORR	Office of Refugee Resettlement
PRM	Bureau of Population, Refugees, and Migration
State	Department of State

Congressional Requesters

Millions of people worldwide have fled their countries because they have been persecuted—or fear being persecuted—on the basis of their race, religion, nationality, political opinions, or because they belong to a particular social group.

The United States has traditionally provided refuge to such people, and continues to resettle at least half of all refugees referred for resettlement worldwide by the United Nations High Commissioner for Refugees each year. In fiscal year 2011, the United States resettled a little more than 56,000 refugees into communities throughout the country. [1]

Nine national voluntary agencies—the nongovernmental organizations that carry out much of the refugee resettlement process with funding from the Departments of State (State) and Health and Human Services (HHS)—take the lead in determining where refugees will initially be placed, with approval from State. The communities in which refugees are placed vary significantly in size, capacity, and experience in resettling refugees. Major gateway cities tend to have more experience incorporating large and steady streams of people from other countries, but can be very expensive places to live.

Smaller cities and towns, on the other hand, can be more affordable and easier to navigate, but may not have sufficient resources to provide refugees adequate services, including education and health care. While some refugees stay in the community where they were initially resettled, others may decide to move to another community that may or may not have organizations and programs to help them become self-sufficient.

The most recent economic downturn has made it increasingly difficult for refugees to become self-sufficient within months of arriving in the United States, raising questions about refugee placement and integration, as well as the oversight of refugee resettlement programs.

In this context, we were asked to examine (1) the factors resettlement agencies consider when determining where refugees are initially placed; (2) the effects refugees have on their communities; (3) how federal agencies ensure the effectiveness and integrity of refugee resettlement programs; and (4) what is known about refugees' integration into the United States.

To address our research objectives, we reviewed relevant federal and state laws, regulations, monitoring protocols, performance reports, performance measures, and other relevant documents. We also conducted a literature review of academic research on the integration of refugees into the United States[2] and reviewed other pertinent reports.

We met with federal agency officials, national voluntary agency staff, and experts on refugee programs. In addition, we conducted site visits to eight communities, where we met with representatives from state and local government entities, voluntary agency affiliates, community-based organizations, local businesses, and other relevant individuals and groups, including refugees.[3] For our site visits, we selected Boise, Idaho; Chicago, Illinois; Detroit, Michigan; Fargo, North Dakota; Knoxville, Tennessee; Lancaster, Pennsylvania; Owensboro, Kentucky; and Seattle, Washington.[4] These eight communities represent a nongeneralizable sample that was selected to include geographically distributed communities with variations in their population sizes, levels of experience resettling refugees, and racial and ethnic diversity. In addition to these factors, several communities were selected because they are considered examples of best practices in refugee resettlement by federal officials. For additional information on our scope and methodology, see appendix I.

We conducted this performance audit from May 2011 through July 2012 in accordance with generally accepted government auditing standards. Those standards require that we plan and perform the audit to obtain sufficient, appropriate evidence to provide a reasonable basis for our findings and conclusions based on our audit objectives. We believe that the evidence obtained provides a reasonable basis for our findings and conclusions based on our audit objectives.

BACKGROUND

A refugee is generally defined as a person who is outside his or her country and who is unable or unwilling to return because of persecution or a well-founded fear of persecution on account of race, religion, nationality, membership in a particular social group, or political opinion.[5] The Refugee Act of 1980, which amended the Immigration and Nationality Act, provided a systematic and permanent procedure for admitting refugees to the United States and maintains comprehensive and uniform provisions to resettle refugees as quickly as possible and to encourage them to become self-sufficient.[6] Several federal, state, and local government agencies coordinate with private organizations to implement the admission and resettlement process.

Refugee Placement in the United States

Each year the President, after appropriate consultation with the Congress and certain Cabinet members, determines the maximum number of refugees the United States may admit for resettlement in a given year.[7] The number actually resettled is typically below this maximum number and has varied over time—sometimes due to security concerns (see fig. 1).[8]

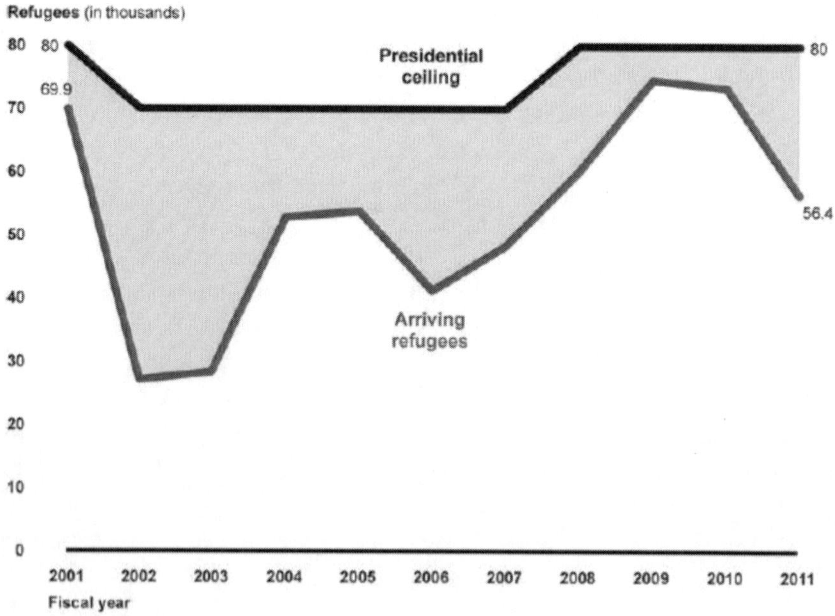

Source: GAO analysis of data from Department of State Refugee Processing Center.

Figure 1. Presidential Ceilings and Refugee Arrivals (FY 2001-2011).

The federal government gives private, voluntary agencies responsibility to determine where refugees will live in the United States, with approval from the Department of State. Refugees are assigned first to a national voluntary agency and then the voluntary agency decides where the refugee will live.[9] More specifically, the nine national voluntary agencies, which maintain a network of about 350 affiliates in communities throughout much of the United States, meet weekly to allocate individual refugees based on an annual evaluation of the communities' capacity to serve refugees.[10] See figure 2 for the number of refugees that arrived in each state during fiscal year 2011.

Appendix III provides additional detail about the countries of origin for arrivals to the 20 states with the largest refugee populations.

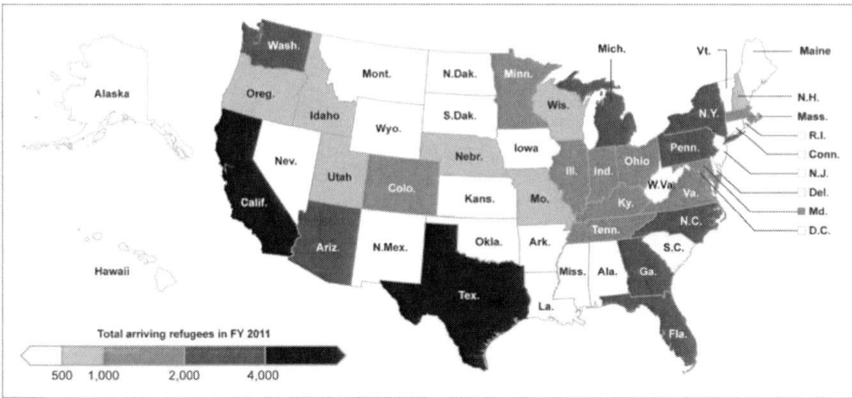

Source: GAO analysis of data from Department of State Refugee Processing Center; National Atlas (base map).

Figure 2. Refugee Arrivals by State (FY 2011).

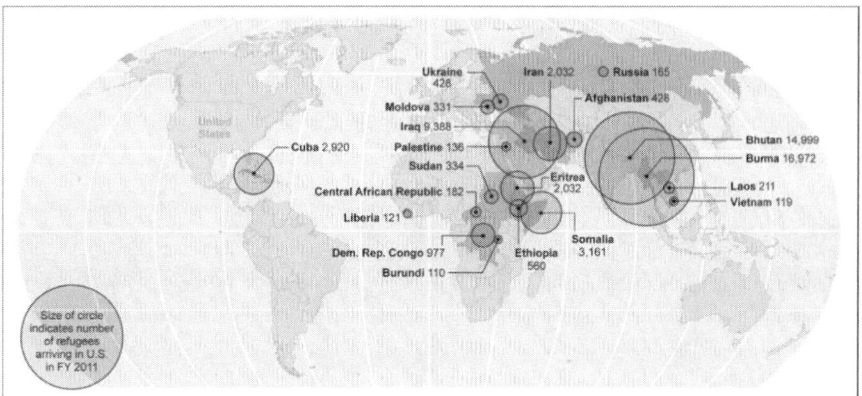

Source: GAO analysis of data from Department of State Refugee Processing Center; National Atlas (base map).

Figure 3. Top 20 Countries of Origin for Refugees Arriving FY 2011.

In the last 10 years, refugees have come to the United States from an increasing number of countries, and the issues associated with these diverse populations have become more complex. For example, many refugees today arrive after having lived in refugee camps for years, and may have little formal education or work experience, or untreated medical or mental health conditions. In turn, receiving communities have needed to adjust their language capabilities and services in order to respond to the changing needs of these diverse refugee populations. Figure 3 shows the top 20 countries of origin for refugees arriving in the United States in fiscal year 2011.

Federal Structure for Refugee Resettlement Programs

Three federal agencies are involved in the refugee resettlement process. The Department of Homeland Security (DHS) approves refugees for admission to the United States. State's Bureau of Population, Refugees, and Migration (PRM) is responsible for processing refugees overseas. Once refugees are processed and arrive in the United States, PRM partially funds services to meet their immediate needs. PRM enters into cooperative agreements with national voluntary agencies under its Reception and Placement Program to provide funding that helps refugees settle into their respective communities during their initial 30 to 90 days and covers housing, food, clothing, and other necessities. Each local affiliate receives $1,850 per refugee to provide these services.[11] Figure 4 illustrates the general path of refugee resettlement in the United States.

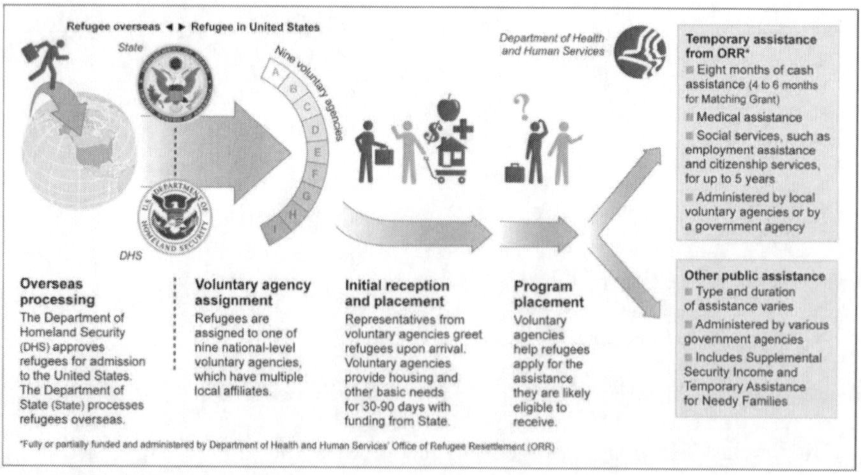

Source: GAO; National Atlas (globe).

Figure 4. General Path of Refugee Resettlement in the United States.

Many refugees are then eligible to receive temporary resettlement assistance from the Office of Refugee Resettlement (ORR), located within HHS. In most states, ORR funds cash and medical assistance as well as social services to help refugees become economically self-sufficient. [12] ORR provides these funds through grants to state refugee coordinators, who may be employed by a state agency or by a nonprofit organization depending on how a state's program is set up.[13] ORR's social services grants provide funding for employment and other support services. States also receive funding from ORR to award discretionary grants—including school impact, services to older refugees, and targeted assistance grants—to communities that are particularly affected by large numbers of refugees or to serve specific refugee populations such as the elderly. See table 1 for a list of selected refugee assistance programs.

In addition, communities may apply for grants from other nonrefugee programs to help provide services to refugees. Both PRM and ORR monitor the implementation of the refugee resettlement process, which involves overseeing and monitoring both government agencies and private organizations (see fig. 5).

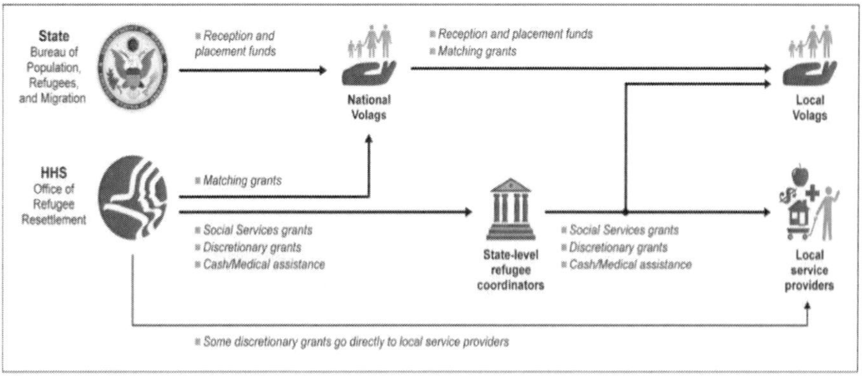

Source: GAO.

Figure 5. Flow of Funds from PRM and ORR to Service Providers.

ORR and PRM officials coordinate with one another and with national and state stakeholders who specifically focus on serving refugees. Together with representatives from national resettlement agencies and state refugee coordinators, ORR and PRM also participate in a refugee resettlement working group convened by the White House National Security Staff, which supports both the Homeland Security Council and the National Security Council. The resettlement working group has worked on and been supportive of a variety of reforms that PRM and ORR have made to their processes. PRM and ORR also conduct joint quarterly consultation meetings with stakeholder groups, including voluntary agencies, state refugee coordinators, refugee health coordinators, ORR technical assistance providers, and ethnic community based organizations.

Table 1. Selected Refugee Assistance Programs[a]

Activities	Purpose	FY 2012 budget authority[a] (in millions)
Reception and placement grants	Provides partial financial support to nongovernmental organizations to provide services to refugees for 30 to 90 days after arrival in the United States, including basic needs, orientation, and case management services	$153.7
Transitional and medical services	Provides cash and medical assistance to refugees, asylees, entrants, trafficking victims, and special immigrant visa holders who participate in certain ORR-funded programs.	323.2
Social services	Supports employment and other services such as social adjustment, translation, child care, and citizenship services as well as case management	118.9
Targeted assistance	Primarily provides services designed to secure employment for refugees within 1 year or less in counties that are impacted by high arrival numbers and high concentrations of refugees	24.2
Preventive health	Promotes refugee access to health screening, assessment, treatment, and follow-up services	4.7

Sources: PRM and HHS Administration for Children and Families Justification of Estimates for Appropriations Committees, fiscal year 2013.

[a]ORR also funds targeted grants for unaccompanied alien children, victims of torture, and victims of trafficking. According to ORR, fiscal year 2012 funding levels reflect the reallocation of funding during FY 2012 to support the costs associated with the unprecedented level of Unaccompanied Alien Children referred to HHS/ORR by the Department of Homeland Security during FY 2012.

VOLUNTARY AGENCIES CONSIDER VARIOUS FACTORS IN PLACING REFUGEES, BUT FEW CONSULT WITH LOCAL SERVICE PROVIDERS

Voluntary Agencies Consider Various Factors When Making Refugee Placement Decisions

Voluntary agencies consider a variety of factors when they propose the number of refugees to be resettled in each community (see table 2). Before preparing their annual proposals for PRM's Reception and Placement Program for approval, national voluntary agencies ask local voluntary agency affiliates to assess their own capacity and that of other service providers in the wider community and propose the number of refugees that they will be able to resettle that year.[14] In making these assessments, local voluntary agency affiliates typically consider both their own internal capacity and the capacity of the community, with different levels of emphasis on one or the other.[15] For example, when determining how many refugees their community can accommodate, local affiliates in one community told us that they primarily consider their internal capacity—such as staffing levels, staff skills, long-term funding needs, the number of refugees they have served in the past, and success in meeting refugee employment goals in the previous year. Local affiliates in another community explained that they primarily consider community-based factors, such as housing availability and employment opportunities. To help make this process more consistent, Refugee Council USA, a coalition of the nine national voluntary agencies, developed guidance and a list of factors that local affiliates could use when evaluating community capacity. However, national voluntary agencies do not require their local affiliates to use the guidance. Moreover, national voluntary agencies may adjust the numbers proposed by local affiliates.

Because refugees are generally placed in communities where national voluntary agency affiliates have been successful in resettling refugees, the same communities are often asked to absorb refugees year after year. One state refugee coordinator noted that local affiliate funding is based on the number of refugees they serve, so affiliates have an incentive to maintain or increase the number of refugees they resettle each year rather than allowing the number to decrease.

Table 2. Sample Factors That Voluntary Agencies Consider When Assessing Community Capacity

Community factors	Internal factors
Employment opportunities	Language ability of staff
Availability of affordable housing	Staff size (ratio of staff to refugees)
Existing ethnic and linguistic groups	Number of Matching Grant program slots
Public transportation	Volunteer corps
Health care resources	Private revenue
State budget trends for public assistance	Long-term financial needs of the organization
Number of available co-sponsors	

Source: GAO analysis of PRM, Refugee Council USA guidance, and interviews with voluntary agency officials.

Given Limited Guidance, Few Voluntary Agencies We Visited Sought Input from Relevant Community Stakeholders When Placing Refugees

Even though they are required to coordinate and consult with state and local governments about their resettlement activities, voluntary agencies have received only limited guidance from PRM on how to obtain input from these and other community stakeholders when assessing communities' capacity. The Immigration and Nationality Act, as amended, states that it is the intent of Congress that local voluntary agency activities should be conducted in close cooperation and advance consultation with state and local governments,[16] and the cooperative agreements that the Department of State enters into with national voluntary agencies require the agencies to conduct their reception and placement activities in this manner.[17] Driven by concerns that voluntary agencies were not consulting sufficiently with state and local stakeholders when developing their proposals, PRM directed local voluntary agencies to do more to document consultations with state and local stakeholders regarding the communities' capacity to serve refugees.[18] However, PRM's guidance on consultation with state and local governments does not provide detailed information regarding the agency's expectations for the content of these discussions. While the guidance provides some examples of state and local stakeholders that the voluntary agencies could potentially consult, it does not state which stakeholders must be consulted. PRM officials said that they allow local voluntary agencies to decide whom to consult because the voluntary agencies know their communities best and because local circumstances vary.

Most local voluntary agencies we visited have not taken steps to ensure that other relevant service providers are afforded the opportunity to provide input on the number and types of refugees that can be served. As a result, many local service providers experienced challenges in properly serving refugees. Most of the local voluntary agencies told us they generally consult with private stakeholders such as apartment landlords or potential employers prior to resettling refugees in an area. They also stated that they consult with some public entities, such as state refugee coordinators; however, most public entities such as public schools and health departments generally said that voluntary agencies notified them of the number of refugees expected to arrive in the coming year, but did not consult them regarding the number of refugees they could serve before proposals were submitted to PRM. Moreover, service providers in one community noted that because the local voluntary agencies did not consult them on the numbers and ethnicities of refugees they were planning to resettle, there were no interpreters or residents that spoke the language of some of the refugees who were resettled there, even though the providers could have served refugees that spoke other languages.

Voluntary agencies may not consult with relevant stakeholders if they perceive them to be unaware of the resettlement process or if they believe that refugees do not use certain services. For example, local voluntary agency staff in one community said they did not consult with certain stakeholders because they believed that they were not well informed about the resettlement process and might unnecessarily object to the proposed number of refugees to be resettled. In fact, one local, elected official we spoke to was unaware that refugees were living in the community. Other elected officials noted that it was difficult to tell if or when refugees accessed services, even though school and health department officials in those same communities had frequent interactions with refugees and wanted opportunities to provide input.

Although they bear much of the responsibility for providing services to refugees, some of the health care providers and schools that had not been consulted on, or even notified of, the number of refugees that were to be resettled sometimes felt unprepared to do so. For example, health care providers in two communities told us that they were not notified in advance that refugees would be arriving in their communities, and thus, had no time to set up screening procedures. They were also unaware of the specific needs and health challenges of the communities they were serving.

In addition, in some instances when voluntary agencies were unable to adequately prepare the community as a whole for the new arrivals and provide refugees with the services they needed, some community members expressed opposition toward the refugees. For example, in Fort Wayne, Indiana, a few case studies show that the community, which had been receiving fewer than 500 refugees per year prior to 2007, experienced a rapid increase that more than tripled the number of refugees resettled in the community.[19] The community, in turn, was forced on short notice to obtain new sources of funding and establish a new infrastructure in order to serve their new arrivals. This unplanned increase in refugees, combined with a growing unemployment rate, engendered frustrations that resulted in backlash from the community. Moreover, a number of other factors, including the high frequency of communicable diseases among certain populations, unmet needs for mental health services, overcrowding in homes, and cultural practices caused existing residents to become concerned or even hostile. Similarly, officials in Clarkston, Georgia, another community that was not initially consulted regarding the resettlement of thousands of refugees beginning in 1996, described the flight of long-time residents from the town in response to refugee resettlement and the perceived deterioration of the quality of schools.[20]

In a few of the communities we visited, after reaching a crisis point due to the influx of refugees, stakeholders took the initiative to develop formal processes for providing input to the local voluntary agencies on the number of refugees they could serve.[21] For example, an influx of refugees in Fargo, North Dakota, in the 1990s overwhelmed local service providers. In response, those service providers and the local voluntary agency formed a Refugee Advisory Committee to provide a formal, community-based structure for finding solutions to challenges in resettling refugees. The committee includes representatives from the local voluntary agency, state and county social services departments, various city departments, school districts, as well as local health care providers, nonprofit organizations, and the assistant state refugee coordinator. The local voluntary agency solicits input from the committee annually on the number of refugees the community has the capacity to serve in the coming year and also meets quarterly to address other issues such as the needs of service providers. Committee members told us that the number of new refugees arriving in Fargo declined after the committee was developed.[22] Committee members and voluntary agency officials said that their close communication allows them to better educate the community and better serve the refugees, and both believe the number being resettled is manageable. Similarly, in Boise, Idaho, city officials formed a roundtable group to develop a Refugee Resource Strategic Community Plan in 2009 to work with the local voluntary agencies, the state refugee coordinator's office, and community organizations to identify strategies for successful resettlement of Boise's refugees, in light of the most recent economic downturn. The group includes representatives from the state coordinator's office, local voluntary agencies, various city departments, school district representatives, nonprofit organizations, as well as employers, health care providers, and other community stakeholders. The group meets quarterly to review progress on the objectives outlined in the strategic plan. The local voluntary agencies obtain input from the group members on the community's capacity for serving refugees, but they do not discuss the specific number of refugees that will be proposed to the national voluntary agency and PRM for resettlement. Roundtable members told us that the local voluntary agencies have worked with their national offices to reduce the proposed number of refugees to resettle in Boise in 2011 based on community capacity.

The state of Tennessee has passed legislation that creates formal processes for communication between voluntary agencies and local stakeholders. Specifically, the Refugee Absorptive Capacity Act,[23] which was passed in 2011, requires the state refugee program office to enter into a letter of agreement with each voluntary agency in the state. The letter of agreement must contain a requirement that local stakeholders mutually consult and prepare a plan for the initial placement of refugees in a community as well as a plan for ongoing consultation. In addition, the state program office must ensure that local voluntary agencies consult upon request with local governments regarding refugee placement in advance of the refugees' arrival.[24]

Refugees Bring Benefits to Communities but Can Pose Challenges for Service Providers

Refugees Bring Diversity and Can Help Stimulate Development, but Can Stretch Resources and Affect Program Outcomes

Communities can benefit socially and economically from refugee resettlement. In all of the communities we visited, stakeholders said that refugees enriched their cultural diversity. For example, local service providers in Fargo commented that refugees bring new perspectives and customs to a city with predominately Norwegian ancestry. Some city officials and business leaders we spoke with in several communities said that refugees help stimulate economic development by filling critical labor shortages as well as by starting small businesses and creating jobs. For instance, new refugee-owned businesses revitalized a neighborhood in Chicago after other businesses in the area closed. In addition, an official in Washington State told us that diverse resettlement communities with international populations attract investment from overseas businesses. According to ORR officials, refugees also bring economic benefits to communities by renting apartments, patronizing local businesses, and paying taxes, and the presence of refugees may increase the amount of federal funding that a community receives.[25] In Boise, officials commented that the refugee students helped stabilize the public school population, which had been declining before the city established a refugee resettlement program. While refugees can benefit their communities, they can also stretch the resources of local service providers, such as school districts and health care systems. In several communities we visited, school district officials said that it takes more resources to serve refugee students than nonrefugee students, because they sometimes lack formal schooling or have experienced trauma, which can require additional supports, such as special training for school staff. In addition, newly arrived refugee students often have limited English proficiency, and hiring interpreters can be costly.[26] Similarly, some health care providers expressed concerns about serving refugees, because they said that they are required to provide interpreter services to patients with limited English proficiency.[27] One provider told us that their clinic spent more than $100,000 on interpreter services in the previous year, costs that were not reimbursed.[28] In addition, in some communities we visited, school district officials and health care providers said that locating interpreters for certain languages can be difficult. ORR and PRM officials noted that these impacts are not unique to refugees and that serving immigrants may pose similar challenges. ORR offers discretionary grants to assist school districts that serve a large number of refugees, but we learned that district officials may be unaware of these grants or may decide that the effort involved in applying for them outweighs the potential benefits. For example, through its school impact grant, ORR funds activities for refugee students such as English as a Second Language instruction and after-school tutorials. However, school district officials in one community that was new to the refugee resettlement program said they had no information about where they could find assistance in serving refugee students. In another community, district officials were aware of the school impact grant, but said they did not apply for it because they found the application process to be burdensome and the funding level would have been insufficient to meet their needs.[29] In addition to stretching school district resources, refugee students can also negatively affect district performance outcomes. School district performance is measured primarily by students' test scores, including the scores of refugee students. School district officials in several communities said that even though refugee students often have limited English proficiency, they are evaluated against the same metrics as their native English-speaking peers, which can result in lower performance outcomes for the district. In one community, officials told us that the district had not demonstrated adequate yearly progress under the state standards in recent years, and they attributed this in part to the test scores of refugee students.[30] Furthermore, refugees who exhaust federal refugee assistance benefits and are not self-sufficient can strain local safety nets. Refugees who are no longer eligible to receive cash and medical assistance from ORR after 8 months but are unemployed—or are working in low-wage jobs that do not provide sufficient income—may seek help from local service providers such as food pantries, organizations providing housing assistance, and even homeless shelters. If service providers are unprepared to serve these refugees in addition to their other clients, it can stretch their budgets and diminish the safety net resources available to others in the community. Table 3 lists the benefits and challenges of refugee resettlement identified by stakeholders in the communities we visited.

Table 3. Benefits and Challenges of Refugee Resettlement Identified in Site Visits

Benefits	Challenges
Refugees add diversity to their communities The presence of refugees in a community teaches tolerance for others Refugees take jobs that are difficult to fill Refugees are reliable, dedicated employees Refugee-owned businesses create jobs Public services developed to assist refugees, such as transit programs, also benefit other vulnerable populations	Communication can be difficult due to language and cultural barriers Mental health resources are limited for refugees who have experienced trauma The cost of interpreter services can strain service providers' budgets, and some healthcare providers have chosen to stop serving refugees Refugee students with limited English proficiency can affect school districts' performance outcomes Some refugees live in poverty due to unemployment Some refugees are unfamiliar with social norms and laws in the United States

Source: GAO interviews with stakeholders in selected communities.

Some Refugees Relocate after Resettlement, and This Secondary Migration May Strain Communities That Lack Adequate Resources to Serve Them

Migration from one community to another after initial resettlement—referred to as secondary migration—can unexpectedly increase the refugee population in a community, and communities that attract large numbers of secondary migrants may not have adequate, timely funding to provide resettlement services to the migrants who need them.[31]

According to ORR, refugees relocate for a variety of reasons: better employment opportunities, the pull of an established ethnic community, more welfare benefits, better training opportunities, reunification with relatives, or a more congenial climate.[32] Not all refugees who migrate choose to access resettlement services in their new communities, according to PRM officials. However, for those migrants who need resettlement services, federal funding does not necessarily follow them to their new communities, even though refugees continue to be eligible for some resettlement services for 5 years after arrival. According to ORR officials, refugees who relocate while they are receiving cash assistance, medical assistance, or refugee social services are eligible to continue receiving those services in their new communities for a limited time.[33] However, ORR does not coordinate this continuation of service, and state refugee coordinators must communicate with one another to determine eligibility for each refugee who relocates.

In addition, ORR provides grants to communities and states affected by secondary migration, but the annual cycle of these grants may not provide ORR the flexibility to respond in a timely manner. ORR uses secondary migration data submitted by states once a year, among other data, to inform refugee social services funding allocations for future fiscal years. 34 According to ORR officials, these formula grants are awarded annually to states based on the number of refugee arrivals during the previous 2 years. As a result, a year may pass before states experiencing secondary migration receive increased funding. For example, Minnesota reported to ORR that 1,999 refugees migrated into the state during fiscal year 2010, but under ORR's current formula funding process, the state would not have received increased funding until fiscal year 2011. In another example, social services funding did not keep pace with a large number of arrivals of both newly resettled refugees and secondary migrants in Detroit in fiscal year 2008. According to a report commissioned by ORR, after this rapid influx of arrivals, caseloads rose to 150 clients per caseworker in the employment and training program, and caseworkers were forced to devote a majority of their time to paperwork and case management, which limited their ability to provide job development and training services.[35] Further, ORR will not adjust a state's level of social services funding to account for secondary migration until it verifies that the refugees migrated to the state. According to one state refugee coordinator, ORR rejects the data states submit if the refugee's information does not match the information in ORR's database or if two or more states claim to have served the same refugee. ORR officials said that, while their process allows states to update missing data and correct formatting errors, it does not allow states to resubmit data that does not match the information in ORR's database or that was submitted by two or more states.[36]

ORR offers supplemental, short-term funding to help communities affected by secondary migration. For example, the Supplemental Services for Recently Arrived Refugees grant is designed to help communities provide services to secondary migrants or newly arriving refugees when the communities are not sufficiently prepared in terms of linguistic or culturally appropriate services or do not have sufficient service capacity. However, this grant is only available to communities that will serve a minimum of 100 refugees annually, and the funding is for a fixed period of time.[37] Communities must apply and be approved for the grant, and funding may not arrive until many months after the influx began. For example, in a draft report on secondary migration commissioned by ORR, the Spring Institute for Intercultural Learning found that one community did not receive supplemental funding until 14 months after secondary migrant refugees began arriving.[38]

Without comprehensive secondary migration data, ORR cannot target supplemental assistance to communities and refugees in a timely way. Currently, the data that PRM and ORR collect on secondary migration are limited and little is known about secondary migration patterns. PRM collects data from local voluntary agencies regarding the number of refugees who move away from a community within the first 90 days after arrival, but does not collect data on the estimated number of refugees who enter the community during the same time period. PRM officials said that they use these out-migration data to assess the success of refugee placement decisions. In contrast, ORR collects secondary migration data annually from each state, but does not collect community-level data. Specifically, ORR collects information on the number of refugees who move into and out of each state every year. However, ORR officials explained that they can only collect these data when secondary migrants access services. As a result, refugees who move into or out of a state but do not use refugee services in their new communities are not counted. Even so, these refugees access other community services and their communities may need additional assistance to meet their needs.

Secondary migration can strain local resources significantly. For example, the draft report on secondary migration prepared for ORR by the Spring Institute for Intercultural Learning found that refugees who migrate to new communities can overwhelm local service providers, such as health departments, that are unprepared to serve them. In addition, a report prepared for ORR by General Dynamics Information Technology, Inc. found that, in one community, the influx of a large number of secondary migrants who lacked resources led to a homelessness crisis that stressed the capacity of both the shelter system and the other agencies serving refugees.[39]

Capacity Challenges Can Lead Communities to Request Restrictions or Temporary Moratoriums on Refugee Resettlement

Some communities that face challenges in serving additional refugees have requested restrictions or even temporary moratoriums on refugee resettlement. According to PRM, the cities of Detroit and Fort Wayne, Indiana, requested restrictions on refugee resettlement due to poor economic conditions. In response, PRM limited resettlement in Detroit and Fort Wayne to refugees who already have family there.[40] In addition, the mayor of Manchester, New Hampshire, asked in 2011 that PRM temporarily stop resettling refugees in the city because of a shortage of jobs and sufficient affordable housing. While PRM did not grant the requested moratorium, the agency reduced the number of refugees to be resettled there in fiscal year 2011 from 300 to about 200. PRM officials said that a moratorium on resettlement would not have made sense because nearly all of the refugees slated to be resettled in Manchester have family there and would likely relocate to Manchester eventually— even if they were initially settled in another location.

Tennessee recently created a process by which communities could request a temporary moratorium on refugee resettlement for capacity reasons. The state's Refugee Absorptive Capacity Act allows local governments to submit a request to the state refugee office for a 1-year moratorium on resettling additional refugees if they document that they lack the capacity to do so and if further resettlement would have an adverse impact on residents. The state refugee office may then forward this request to PRM. 41 Passed in 2011, the law states that local governments should consider certain capacity factors—the capacity of service providers to meet existing needs of current residents, the availability of affordable housing, the capacity of the school district to meet the needs of refugee students, and the ability of the local economy to absorb new workers—before making such a request. According to PRM, to date, no community in Tennessee has submitted such a request.

Agencies Monitor Resettlement and Measure Effectiveness, but These Measures Have Weaknesses

PRM and ORR Take Different Approaches to Program Oversight

PRM conducts regular on-site monitoring of national voluntary agencies and about 350 local affiliates to ensure that the voluntary agencies deliver the services outlined in their cooperative agreements. Under the cooperative agreements, local voluntary agencies must provide certain services to refugees in the first 30 to 90 days after they arrive. PRM monitors national voluntary agencies annually and local affiliates once every 5 years, and requires national voluntary agencies to monitor their affiliates at least once every 3 years. During its local affiliate monitoring visits, PRM reviews case files and interviews staff. PRM officials also visit a small sample of refugees in their homes to ensure that the refugees received clean, safe housing and appropriate furniture. PRM also requires voluntary agencies to report certain outcome measures for each refugee they resettle.

In recent years, PRM found most local affiliates generally compliant, and for those that were not, PRM made recommendations and required immediate corrective action. For fiscal years 2009 through 2011, according to PRM, it conducted 136 on-site monitoring visits. In over three-quarters of those visits, PRM determined that the local affiliate was compliant or mostly compliant. In about one-quarter of the cases, however, PRM determined that they were partially or mostly noncompliant (about 20 percent) or simply noncompliant (about 5 percent). PRM or national resettlement agencies can make return, on-site monitoring trips to assess the progress of affiliates when problems are identified. Furthermore, if the problems persist, national voluntary agencies can close an affiliate's operation or PRM can decide not to allow placement of refugees at an affiliate. For fiscal year 2011, PRM determined that the most common recommendation made to local affiliates was that the local affiliate should document the reason core services could not be provided in the required time frames. (See table 4 for the top 10 recommendations made for fiscal year 2011.)

Table 4. Top 10 Recommendations for FY 2011 from PRM Monitoring Visits

1. Ensure that when core services cannot be completed within the time frames specified in the Cooperative Agreement, the case note logs specify the reason for the delay.
2. Ensure that services are provided with interpretation, as needed, that allows for communication with the refugee in his/her native language or in a common language in which the refugee is fluent, throughout the reception and placement period.
3. Take immediate steps to ensure that infestation noted in home visits is addressed.
4. Conduct at least two home visits for each case: the initial home visit within 24 hours,as well as an additional home visit within 30 days of arrival.
5. Ensure that refugees receive all essential furnishings upon arrival.
6. Ensure that a resettlement plan is developed for each refugee, including children, that indicates the initial assessment of employability for each employable refugee and includes a clear plan of action based on an assessment of the individual.
7. The headquarters should have in place a formal plan for training new headquarters staff and affiliate directors, and should ensure that each affiliate has a structured training plan for each of its new employees.
8. The affiliate should ensure that culturally appropriate, ready-to-eat food is available upon a refugee's arrival, plus one day's worth of additional food supplies. The affiliate should provide food or food allowance at least equivalent to the food stamp allocation continued food assistance until receipt of food stamps or until the individual or family is able to provide his or her own food.
9. Ensure minor suitability determinations are completed within 1 week of the minor's arrival, and that minors' files are segregated and can be readily identified.
10. Ensure that every refugee has a health assessment within 30 days of arrival and that refugees with acute health care requirements receive appropriate and timely medical attention.

Source: PRM.

Whereas PRM's oversight focuses on services provided, ORR's oversight focuses more on performance outcomes. In order to assess the performance of its programs that provide cash, medical assistance, and social services to refugees, ORR monitors employment outcomes and cash assistance terminations (see table 5). It uses a similar set of measures for its Matching Grant program.

Table 5. Performance Outcome Measures for Major Refugee Assistance Programs

Statewide Measures[a]	Matching Grant program
1. Entered Employment	1. Entered Employment
2. Average Wage at Employment	2. Average Wage at Employment
3. Employment with Health Benefits	3. Employment with Health Benefits
4. Job Retention for 90 days	4. Self-Sufficient at 120th day
5. Cash Assistance Reductions due to Earnings	5. Economic Self-Sufficiency Retention at the180th day
6. Cash Assistance Termination due to Earnings	6. Economic Self-Sufficiency Overall

Source: ORR program guidance.

[a]ORR prepares an Annual Performance Plan, which presents goals and progress toward six measures of economic self-sufficiency. Each state negotiates with ORR to establish a target for each measure, and states are encouraged to set or negotiate similar targets with programs within the state. ORR uses these measures for all statewide programs—publicly administered, public private partnerships, and Wilson-Fish programs, which are administered by a voluntary agency. For more information on the statewide programs, see GAO-11-369.

According to ORR, its focus on employment outcomes as a measure of effectiveness is based on the Immigration and Nationality Act, as amended, which requires ORR to help refugees attain economic self-sufficiency as soon as possible.[42] ORR considers refugees self-sufficient if they earn enough income that enables the family to support itself without cash assistance—even if they receive other types of noncash public assistance, such as Supplemental Nutrition Assistance Program benefits or Medicaid.[43]

ORR conducts its on-site monitoring at the state level to ensure the program is able to collect and report accurate data and to ensure that the state is able to provide services to refugees. ORR's on-site monitoring identifies deficiencies as well as best practices. ORR generally monitors state refugee coordinators onsite once every 3 years, as the state coordinator is responsible for administering and overseeing ORR's major grants. During the on-site visit, ORR also monitors a sample of subgrantees. In monitoring reports from its most recent on-site monitoring in the states we visited, ORR identified a number of deficiencies including:

- failure to inform refugees that they were eligible for certain services for up to 5 years,
- failure to ensure that medical assistance was terminated at the end of the 8-month eligibility period,
- failure to ensure that translators were available when providing services to refugees, and
- missing documentation in case files.

The monitoring reports contained ORR's recommendations and noted when corrective action was required. ORR's monitoring reports also identified program strengths and best practices that monitors observed while on site. For example, one ORR monitoring report noted that having a state refugee housing coordinator was a program strength, because this coordinator can locate affordable housing and research funding sources, which saves the caseworkers time and effort.

In the same state, ORR found that having an employment specialist at a voluntary agency who can help refugees obtain job upgrades and pursue professional certificates was also a program strength. According to ORR officials, they supplement this on-site monitoring with desk monitoring, which may include reviews of case files, or reviews of information provided in periodic reports.

Neither ORR nor PRM has formal mechanisms for collecting and sharing information gleaned during monitoring to improve services, such as solutions to common problems or promising practices. ORR and PRM officials identified some informal mechanisms for sharing such information with service providers, but relied mostly on service providers to network among themselves or share information during quarterly conference calls and annual consultations.

ORR also relies on external technical assistance providers to disseminate best practices when training grantees and expects state refugee coordinators to share findings of monitoring reports with their local partners. However, monitoring reports are not publicly available, and, unless the state coordinators share this information, service providers may not be able to identify promising practices, track monitoring results, identify trends, and address common issues. As a result, service providers do not always get the information they need to improve services, whether by preventing a problem or implementing a best practice.

ORR's Performance Measures Encourage Service Providers to Focus on Short-Term Outcomes

ORR's performance measures focus on short-term outcomes, even though refugees remain eligible for social services funded by ORR for up to 5 years.[44] Because it is important for refugees to become employed before their cash assistance runs out—8 months or less, depending on the service delivery model—ORR's performance measures provide incentives for service providers to focus on helping refugees gain and maintain employment quickly. Specifically, ORR requires grantees to measure entered employment at 6 months for the Matching Grant program or 8 months for statewide cash assistance programs.[45] In addition, ORR requires grantees to measure job retention 90 days after employment. This focus on short-term employment, however, can result in a one-size-fits-all approach to employment services and may, in turn, limit service providers' flexibility to provide services that may benefit refugees after the 6 to 8 month time frame. That is, with limited incentives to focus on longer-term employment and wages, service providers may not help refugees obtain longer-term services and training, such as on-the-job or vocational training, which could significantly boost their income or benefit the refugee in the long-term or after employment is measured.[46] For example, when assisting refugees who arrive with college degrees and professional experience, service providers may not help them earn a credential valid in the United States, because the providers' effectiveness is measured by whether the refugee is employed. Additionally, ORR does not allow skills certification training to exceed 1 year and requires the refugees to be employed when receiving training and services.[47] Several service providers mentioned this as a challenge for highly skilled Iraqi refugees, in particular, some of whom include doctors and engineers.[48]

In addition, voluntary agency officials noted that ORR's employment measures do not allow them to report on the longer-term or nonemployment-related outcomes of the other refugee resettlement services they provide. As a result, services such as skills training, English language training, or mental health services—which provide longer-term benefits and benefits unrelated to employment—may not be emphasized. According to some local voluntary agency officials we spoke to, given the current performance measures, there is a disincentive to dedicate necessary time and resources to the nonemployment activities that create pathways to success for refugees. It may be particularly difficult to serve those who do not arrive in the United States ready to work due to trauma, illness, or lack of basic skills.

While much of ORR's grant funding focuses on short-term employment, ORR does have some discretionary grants that provide funding for particular purposes that may include services that focus on longer-term goals or more intensive case management. For example, the individual development account program provides matching funds to help refugees save money for the purchase of a vehicle or a home.[49] For these relatively small competitively awarded discretionary grant programs, ORR gathers data on how much money was saved and what assets were purchased, but does not gather data on how these asset purchases affected earnings or self-sufficiency. Descriptions of discretionary grants that can be used to fund services beyond the initial resettlement period, as well as other selected ORR and PRM grant programs, can be found in appendix IV.

In addition to the employment measures' focus on short term outcomes, one state coordinator also noted that these employment measures leave room for interpretation. Specifically, some voluntary agencies may have a narrow definition of employment services while others may have a broader definition. In turn, the percentage of refugees who become employed after receiving employment services could vary based on what types of services are considered employment services. As a result, according to a state coordinator, measures may not provide consistent information about how well a program is performing in different communities.

LITTLE IS KNOWN ABOUT THE EXTENT OF REFUGEE INTEGRATION, BUT STUDIES OFFER A FRAMEWORK FOR ASSESSING INTEGRATION

Federal Agencies Promote but Do Not Currently Measure Refugee Integration

While federal refugee resettlement programs generally provide only short-term assistance, PRM and ORR both aim to prepare refugees for longterm integration into their communities. Although there is no single, generally accepted definition of integration in the literature, integration can be defined as a dynamic, multidirectional process in which newcomers and the receiving communities intentionally work together, based on a shared commitment to acceptance and justice, to create a secure, welcoming, vibrant, and cohesive society.[50] The federal government's efforts to facilitate integration begin before refugees even enter the United States, as PRM offers cultural orientation for all refugees and recently piloted English language training for refugees in certain overseas locations.[51] According to PRM, this cultural orientation and language training is intended to lay the groundwork for refugees' longterm integration into the United States. Integration is also a part of ORR's mission and overall goal,[52] and officials told us that they consider integration to be a central aspect of refugee resettlement. Although ORR only provides refugees with cash and medical assistance for a maximum of 8 months, officials noted that this initial assistance helps set the foundation for long-term integration. Other ORR programs provide longer-term services that are intended to further facilitate integration, but these services may not be as widely available as cash and medical assistance. For example, ORR's social services grant program funds employment services and other support services to refugees for up to 5 years after arrival, but communities may choose to provide these services for a shorter period of time due to local resource constraints. ORR's discretionary grants for micro-enterprise assistance and individual development accounts are also designed to facilitate integration by helping refugees start businesses in the communities where they live, among other goals.[53] However, these discretionary grants are competitively awarded and are thus not available to all communities.

ORR has studied approaches that facilitate refugee integration. In 2006, ORR created an integration working group to identify indicators of refugee integration and ways in which ORR could more fully support the integration process. In a 2007 interim report, the working group made both short-term and long-term recommendations to ORR, including that it (1) consider expanding ORR's discretionary grant programs; (2) focus on integration in the areas of employment, English language acquisition, health, housing, and civic engagement; and (3) identify lessons learned from communities where refugee integration appears to be taking place. ORR officials told us that they have implemented many, but not all, of the working group's recommendations due to funding constraints.[54] For example, ORR commissioned a study to identify promising practices that appear to facilitate integration in four U.S. cities.[55]

Neither PRM nor ORR currently measure refugee integration as a program outcome. According to PRM, it does not measure refugee integration due to the short-term nature of the Reception and Placement Program. While refugee integration is part of ORR's mission and overall goal, ORR officials said they have not measured it because there is no clear definition of integration, because it is unclear when integration should be measured, and because the Refugee Act focuses on self-sufficiency outcomes related to employment.

Even so, ORR officials told us that they collect some data related to refugee integration. Specifically, as part of its annual report to Congress, ORR conducts a survey to gauge refugees' economic self-sufficiency that includes integration-related measures such as employment, English language proficiency, participation in job training, attendance in a high school or university degree or certificate program, and home ownership.[56] However, ORR officials noted that the survey is not designed to measure integration and should not be used for this purpose, especially since there is no clear definition of integration. In addition, the survey has had a low response rate, which may affect the quality of the data.[57]

Studies Offer a Framework for Measuring and Facilitating Integration

Studies on refugee resettlement do not offer a broad assessment of how well refugees have integrated into the United States. Of the 13 studies we identified that addressed refugee integration, almost all were limited in scope in that they focused on particular refugee groups in specific geographic locations.[58] The studies describe the integration experiences of specific refugee groups, including factors that help refugees successfully integrate into their communities. However, because of the studies' limited scope and differences in their methodologies, they provide limited insight into how refugees overall have integrated in the United States or how the experiences of different groups compare to one another.

Although the studies we reviewed were not directly comparable, together they identified a variety of indicators that can be used to assess progress toward integration for both individuals and communities, as well as common facilitators of integration. Indicators of integration include employment, English language acquisition, housing, physical and mental health, and social connections, as well as political involvement, citizenship status, and participation in community organizations. One study noted that when assessing integration, it is important to ask refugees whether they consider themselves to be integrated.

The studies we reviewed also identified a range of barriers to integration. Some frequently cited barriers were a lack of formal education, illiteracy or limited English proficiency, and insufficient income from low-paying jobs. For example, refugees who are illiterate or have limited English proficiency may be limited to low-paying jobs such as hotel housekeepers and may not earn sufficient income to meet their needs. Furthermore, one study found that the timing of employment can be a barrier to integration. Specifically, the study found that taking a job soon after arrival can slow down the acquisition of English language skills because refugees may have less available time to attend language classes.

In addition, the studies we reviewed identified facilitators of integration—circumstances and strategies that can help refugees integrate successfully into their communities. English language acquisition is an important facilitator of integration. For example, one study found that refugees who are proficient in English are better able to connect with nonrefugees in their communities, expanding their social connections and sources of support. Other facilitators of integration included employment, social support from other refugees, and affiliation with or sponsorship by a religious congregation. For example, religious congregations may provide refugees with language classes, social activities, emotional and financial support, and linkages with employment and educational opportunities, medical care, and transportation. See table 6 for additional examples of indicators of integration, barriers to integration, and facilitators of integration.

Table 6. Selected Integration Indicators, Barriers, and Facilitators Identified in Literature Review

Indicators of integration	Barriers to integration	Facilitators of integration
Civic participation	None identified	• Political involvement • Community organizing of refugee groups
Culture	• Unfamiliarity with "Western" culture • Intolerance for non-English speakers • Intolerance for cultural or religious differences	• Availability of public serviceproviders to educate community about refugees' cultures (and vice versa)
Education or training	• Lack of or little formal education prior to arrival in the U.S. • Lack of options for re-credentialing for skilled workers or professionals	•Adulteducation opportunities

Table 6. (Continued)

Indicators of integration	Barriers to integration	Facilitators of integration
Employment	• Insufficient income from low-paying jobs • Workplace environments with no opportunity to speak English	• English proficiency, which may help refugees obtain work that generates sufficient income • Networks and support groups that help refugees find employment • Ethnic small businesses
English language acquisition	• Illiteracy or limited English proficiency • "Work first" emphasis, which may slow language acquisition if it limits time to attend English classes	• Opportunities to learnand practice speaking English • Participation in English classes for an extended period of time
Host community	• Harassment and discrimination • Negative interactions with government entities, creating mistrust • Limited resources of agencies serving refugees	• Preparation of the community to receive newcomers • Bilingual and culturally competent staff at agencies serving refugees • Community events to celebrate refugees' cultures
Housing	• Inadequate housing • Low-income, high-crime neighborhoods • Housing settings with no opportunity to speak English	• Moving out of low-income neighborhoods
Social connections	• Social isolation	• Social support from other refugees • Friendship or mentoring programs • Community dinners and gardens • Affiliation with or sponsorship by a religious congregation

Source: GAO literature review.

Some Communities Have Developed Formal Plans for Refugee Integration

While most of the communities we visited had not established formal goals or strategies to facilitate refugee integration, two of the eight communities had developed formal plans to promote integration. The City of Boise, for example, developed a plan to facilitate the successful resettlement of refugees that includes goals related to integration. Specifically, the plan aims to facilitate integration by (1) establishing refugee community centers, (2) using a media campaign to increase community awareness and support of refugees, and (3) creating a mentoring program for refugee youth, among other things. Similarly, the Village of Skokie, Illinois, a suburb of Chicago, created a strategic plan to help facilitate the integration of immigrants, including refugees, by (1) establishing a coordinating council of key service providers, (2) developing a system to improve providers' access to interpreters, and (3) recruiting and training immigrant and refugee community leaders for government commissions and school boards, among other strategies.

Additionally, in Lancaster, Pennsylvania, Franklin & Marshall College had taken a variety of steps to help facilitate the integration of refugees, including using student volunteers to teach refugees English, tutor refugee students, and help refugee families enroll their children in school and access public health services. In addition, at the time of our visit, the college was partnering with a local voluntary agency affiliate to plan a community conference on refugee integration with the goals of (1) better understanding and addressing the needs of refugees, (2) identifying strategies for fostering rapid integration, and (3) developing a broad coalition of organizations serving refugees that could continue to work together on these issues in the future.

CONCLUSION

Each year, as part of its humanitarian role in the international community, the United States admits tens of thousands of refugees who add richness and diversity to our society but can also have a significant impact on the communities in which they live, particularly in cases where relevant state and local stakeholders are not consulted before refugees are resettled. Advance consultation is important because stakeholders need time to plan so that they can properly serve refugees when they arrive, and because their input on the number of refugees to be resettled can help communities avoid reaching a crisis point. Information about communities that have developed effective strategies for consultation would likely benefit other communities facing similar obstacles.

Without more specific guidance and information on effective strategies for consultation, communities may continue to struggle to meet refugees' needs, which may negatively affect both refugees and their communities and would likely deter integration.

Similarly, while ORR has recognized that some service providers have particularly effective strategies for resettlement, neither ORR nor PRM disseminate this information to other service providers. As a result, not all communities are aware of ways they can do their work more effectively.

Furthermore, while refugees can receive resettlement services for up to 5 years, some find it difficult to access those services when they relocate to another community. In addition, states do not receive increased funding for serving secondary migrants until the year after refugees relocate. As a result, in communities that experience high levels of secondary migration, voluntary agencies and service providers may not have the resources to provide services to the migrants who need them.

Without a funding process that would respond more quickly to localities experiencing high rates of secondary migration, voluntary agencies may have to prioritize serving recently arrived refugees and communities may find their resources for refugees stretched too thin.

As required by the Immigration and Nationality Act, as amended, ORR's programs are designed to help refugees become employed as quickly as possible. ORR's measures of effectiveness, which focus on whether refugees gain employment in the short term, in turn, influence the types of services that refugees receive. Specifically, service providers may choose to provide services that encourage short-term independence from cash assistance, but might not help refugees achieve long-term self-sufficiency.

However, refugees may face unique challenges such as a lack of formal education or work experience, language barriers, and physical and mental health conditions that can make the transition to the United States difficult. Without some incentives to focus on long-term self-sufficiency in addition to short-term independence from cash assistance, refugees may be more likely to need government assistance again in the future, and it may take longer for both refugees and their communities to experience the benefits of integration.

RECOMMENDATIONS FOR EXECUTIVE ACTION

We are making the following four recommendations based on our review:

To help ensure that state and local stakeholders have the opportunity to provide input on the number of refugees resettled in their communities, we recommend that

- the Secretary of State provide additional guidance to resettlement agencies and state coordinators on how to consult with local stakeholders prior to making placement decisions, including with whom to consult and what should be discussed during the consultations; and
- the Secretaries of State and of Health and Human Services collect and disseminate best practices related to refugee placement decisions, specifically on working with community stakeholders, as well as other promising practices from communities.

To assist communities in providing services to secondary migrants, we recommend that the Secretary of Health and Human Services consider additional ways to increase the responsiveness of the grants designed for this purpose. This could include asking states to report secondary migration data more often than once a year, allowing resubmission of secondary migration data from states that was rejected because it did not match ORR's database, creating a process for counting migrants who received services in more than one state, and establishing an emergency grant that could be used to more quickly identify and assist communities that are struggling to serve high levels of secondary migrants. To give service providers more flexibility to serve refugees with different needs and to create incentives to focus on longer term goals, including integration, independence from any government services, and career advancement, we recommend that the Secretary of Health and Human Services examine ORR's performance measures in light of its goals and determine whether changes are needed.

AGENCY COMMENTS AND OUR EVALUATION

We shared a draft of this report with HHS and State for review and comment. In its written comments, HHS generally concurred with our recommendations. Specifically, HHS stated that it supports our recommendation to disseminate best practices, including promising practices from communities, while noting that State and nonprofit community-based and faith-based organizations have traditionally taken the lead on resettling refugees. HHS highlighted the efforts it has made in conducting quarterly placement meetings, which include resettlement agencies and refugee coordinators. While these meetings may be helpful, we believe that HHS can also implement this recommendation by disseminating best practices and program strengths that it documents through its monitoring of states and service providers.

In addition, HHS concurred with our recommendation that it consider additional ways to increase the responsiveness of grants that help communities provide services to secondary migrants, but noted that it already provides Supplemental Services grants, which provide short-term assistance to areas that are impacted by increased numbers of new arrivals or secondary migrants. In addition, it raised concerns that an increase in the frequency of data collection would significantly increase the reporting burden without a mandatory need for the data. HHS also stated that it has a process in place for notifying states of technical problems with population data submitted and allowing them to make corrections. While we recognize that HHS has strategies in place to serve secondary migrants, we continue to believe that (1) the Supplemental Services grants can be improved to be more responsive; (2) more up-to-date population data can help HHS respond more quickly to communities experiencing high levels of secondary migration; and (3) improvements can be made to the process for correcting population data.

HHS also stated that it will consider modifying its performance measures and will also continue to assess the usefulness of data elements collected through required reporting to ensure that the program addresses both self-sufficiency and integration. HHS noted, for example, that it has already begun collecting more information about health through its annual survey of refugees and expanded the number of reporting elements pertaining to health in its program performance reporting form. In addition, it is developing approaches to increase the overall participation rates in its annual survey.

In its written comments, State generally concurred with our recommendations and outlined steps it will take to address them. HHS and State also provided technical comments that were incorporated, as appropriate.

Kay E. Brown
Director, Education, Workforce, and Income Security Issues

Appendix I: Objectives, Scope, and Methodology

To identify the factors resettlement agencies consider when deciding where refugees are initially placed, we reviewed relevant federal and state laws and regulations and other relevant documents, and conducted interviews with federal agency officials and national voluntary agency staff. We interviewed officials from the U.S. Department of State's Bureau of Population, Refugees, and Migration (PRM) and the Department of Health and Human Services' Office of Refugee Resettlement (ORR), as well as representatives from several national voluntary resettlement agencies. We also reviewed documents related to the refugee placement process, such as relevant federal and state laws and regulations, guidance for determining community capacity to resettle refugees, the terms of the cooperative agreements between PRM and national voluntary agencies, and funding opportunity announcements for PRM's Reception and Placement Program. To understand the effects refugees have on their communities, we met with experts on refugee programs and conducted site visits to eight communities across the United States where we met with representatives from state and local government entities, voluntary agency affiliates, community-based organizations, local businesses, and other relevant individuals and groups, including refugees, professors from local universities, and a local church that provided assistance to refugees.[1] For our site visits, we selected Boise, Idaho; Chicago, Illinois; Detroit, Michigan; Fargo, North Dakota; Knoxville, Tennessee; Lancaster, Pennsylvania; Owensboro, Kentucky; and Seattle, Washington.[2] These eight communities represent a nongeneralizable sample that was selected to include geographically distributed communities with variations in their population sizes, levels of experience resettling refugees, and racial and ethnic diversity. In addition to these factors, several communities were selected because they are considered examples of best practices in refugee resettlement by federal officials. All of the selected communities were receiving refugees at the time we visited. We developed site selection criteria based on available literature that discussed factors that influence the impact of refugees on their respective communities and factors that either facilitate or hinder refugee integration. We used these criteria in combination with one another to arrive at a diverse set of communities with varying characteristics. To assess the effectiveness and integrity of refugee resettlement programs, we interviewed federal agency officials, state coordinators, and local voluntary agencies. We also reviewed federal agencies' monitoring plans, protocols and selected monitoring reports for the communities we visited. We reviewed the terms of the cooperative agreements between PRM and national voluntary agencies, as well as reporting guidance, sample performance reports, and performance measures federal agencies use to monitor their programs. To determine what is known about refugees' integration into the United States, we conducted a literature review of academic research on this topic. To identify relevant studies, we conducted searches of various databases including Academic OneFile, EconLit, Education Resources Information Center, National Technical Information Service, PAIS International, PASCAL, ProQuest, PsycINFO, Social Sciences Abstracts, Social Services Abstracts, Social SciSearch, Sociological Abstracts, and WorldCat. We conducted a search using the following criteria, which yielded 18 studies:

- Studies must address the integration of refugees into U.S. communities; [3]
- Studies must have been published from 1995 to the present;
- Studies must be in English; and
- Studies must be scholarly, such as peer-reviewed journal articles.

We performed these searches and identified studies between August 2011 and October 2011. In addition, ORR officials provided us with an ORR-commissioned study of promising practices that appear to facilitate refugee integration, and this study met our selection criteria. To assess the method-logical quality of the 18 studies that met our selection criteria, we evaluated each study's research methodology, including whether the study was original research, the reliability of the data set, if applicable, and the study's findings, assumptions, and limitations. We determined that 13 of the 18 studies were sufficiently reliable for our purposes. We then analyzed the findings of these 13 studies.[4] In addition to conducting a literature review, we met with officials from ORR and PRM to determine what, if any, efforts the federal government has to define, measure, or facilitate refugees' integration into the United States. We discussed refugee integration in our interviews with state and local entities during our site visits. We also reviewed the ORR integration working group's 2007 interim report and ORR's annual reports to Congress. We also obtained secondary migration data from ORR's annual report. We assessed the reliability of this data by interviewing ORR officials knowledgeable about the data. We determined that the data were sufficiently reliable for the purpose of background in this report. We conducted this performance audit from May 2011 through July 2012 in accordance with generally accepted government auditing standards. Those standards require that we plan and perform the audit to obtain sufficient, appropriate evidence to provide a reasonable basis for our findings and conclusions based on our audit objectives. We believe that the evidence obtained provides a reasonable basis for our findings and conclusions based on our audit objectives.

APPENDIX II: STUDIES INCLUDED IN LITERATURE REVIEW

Abu-Ghazaleh, F. "Immigrant Integration in Rural Communities: The Case of Morgan County." *National Civic Review*, vol. 98, no. 1 (2009).

Birman, D., and N. Tran. "Psychological Distress and Adjustment of Vietnamese Refugees in the United States: Association with Pre- and Postmigration Factors." *American Journal of Orthopsychiatry*, vol. 78, no. 1 (2008).

Duchon, D. A. "Home Is Where You Make It: Hmong Refugees in Georgia." *Urban Anthropology*, vol. 26, no. 1 (1997).

Franz, B. "Transplanted or Uprooted? Integration Efforts of Bosnian Refugees Based Upon Gender, Class and Ethnic Differences in New York City and Vienna." *The European Journal of Women's Studies*, vol. 10, no. 2 (2003).

Grigoleit, G. "Coming Home? The Integration of Hmong Refugees from Wat Tham Krabok, Thailand, into American Society." *Hmong Studies Journal*, vol. 7 (2006).

Hume, S.E., and S.W. Hardwick. "African, Russian, and Ukrainian Refugee Resettlement in Portland, Oregon." *The Geographical Review*, vol. 95, no. 2 (2005).

ISED Solutions. Exploring Refugee Integration: Experiences in Four American Communities. A report prepared at the request of the Department of Health and Human Services Office of Refugee Resettlement. June 2010.

Ives, N. "More than a 'Good Back': Looking for Integration in Refugee Resettlement." *Refuge*, vol. 24, no. 2 (2007).

Kenny, P., and K. Lockwood-Kenny. "A Mixed Blessing: Karen Resettlement to the United States." *Journal of Refugee Studies*, vol. 24, no. 2 (2011).

Patil, C.L., M. McGown, P.D. Nahayo, and C. Hadley. "Forced Migration: Complexities in Food and Health for Refugees Resettled in the United States." *NAPA Bulletin*, vol. 34, issue 1 (2010).

Shandy, D., and K. Fennelly. "A Comparison of the Integration Experiences of Two African Immigrant Populations in a Rural Community." *Journal of Religion & Spirituality in Social Work*, vol. 25, no. 1 (2006).

Smith, R.S. "The Case of a City Where 1 in 6 Residents is a Refugee: Ecological Factors and Host Community Adaptation in Successful Resettlement." *American Journal of Community Psychology*, vol. 42, no. 3-4 (2008).

Westermeyer, J.J. "Refugee Resettlement to the United States: Recommendations for a New Approach." *The Journal of Nervous and Mental Disease*, vol. 199, no. 8 (2011).

APPENDIX III: 20 STATES WITH LARGEST NUMBERS OF REFUGEES ARRIVING IN FY 2011 AND REFUGEES' COUNTRIES OF ORIGIN

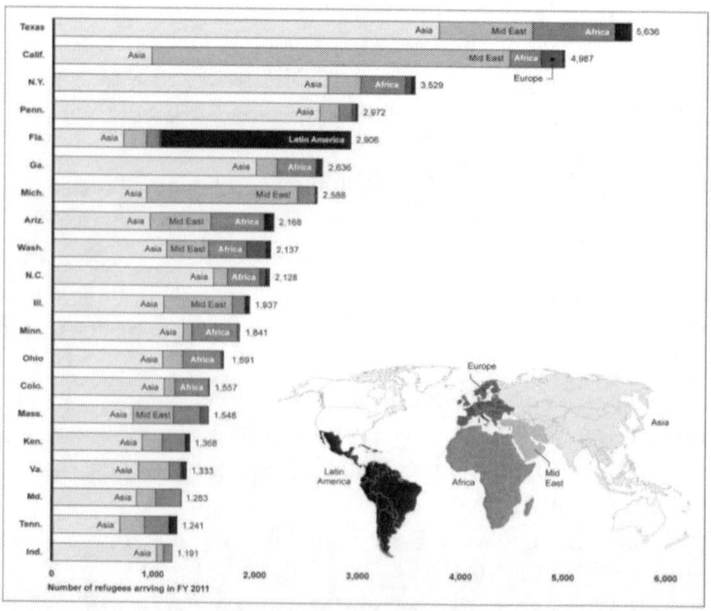

Source: GAO analysis of data from Department of State Refugee Processing Center; National Atlas (world map).

APPENDIX IV: SELECTED PRM AND ORR GRANT PROGRAMS

Agency	Grant	Type	Recipient	Description
PRM	Reception and Placement	Cooperative agreement	National Voluntary Agencies	Provides financial support to partially cover resettlement services based on a fixed per capita sum per refugee resettled in the United States. Services include arrangingfor refugees' placement and providing refugees with basic necessities and core services during their initial resettlement period.
ORR	Refugee Cash and Medical Assistance	Formula	States[a]	Reimburses states and alternative refugee assistance programs for the cost of cash and medical assistance provided to refugees[b]during the first 8 months after their arrival in this country or grant of asylum. It does not provide reimbursement for refugees deemed eligible for Temporary Assistance for Needy Families, SupplementalSecurity Insurance, and Medicaid.
	Voluntary Agency Matching Grant	Cooperative agreement	National Voluntary Agencies	Funds are provided on a matching basis to provide private, nonprofit organizations to fund an alternative to public cash assistance and to support case management, employment services, maintenance assistance, cash allowance, and social services for new arrivals for 4 to 6 months.
	Refugee Social Services	Formula	States	Provides funding for employment and other social services to refugees for 5 years after their data of arrival or grant of asylum.
	Targeted Assistance Grant	Formula	States	Provides funding for employment-related and other social services for refugees in counties with large refugee populations and high refugee concentrations.
	Preventative Health	Discretionary	States and designated health agencies	Provides funds to provide medical screenings to newly arriving refugees, interpreter services, information and referral, and health education.

Appendix IV: (Continued)

Agency	Grant	Type	Recipient	Description
	Targeted Assistance Discretionary	Discretionary	States	Funds to states to implement special employment services not implemented with formula social services grants. Provides funding for employment-related and other social services for refugees in counties with large refugee populations and high refugee concentrations.
	School Impact	Discretionary	States	Provides funds to subcontract with local school systems and nonprofits to support local school systems that are impacted by significant numbers of newly arrived refugeechildren.
	Services to Older Refugees	Discretionary	States	Provide funds to ensure that older refugees will be linked to mainstream aging services in their communities or to provide services directly to older refugees if they are not currently being provided for in the community.
	Preferred Communities Program	Discretionary	National voluntary agencies	The Preferred Communities Program supports the resettlement of newly arriving refugees with the best opportunities for their self-sufficiency and integration into new communities, and supports refugees with special needs that require more intensive case management, culturally and linguistically appropriate linkages and coordination with other service providers to improve their access to services.
	Services for Survivors of Torture	Discretionary	Nonprofit organizations, voluntary agencies, local governments	Provides funding for a comprehensive program of support for survivors of torture, including rehabilitation, social and legal services, and training for providers.

Agency	Grant	Type	Recipient	Description
	Individual Development Account	Discretionary	Nonprofit organizations, voluntary agencies, state and local governments	Funds projects to establish and manage Individual Development Accounts, which are matched savings accounts available for the purchase of specific assets. Matching funds, together with the refugee's own savings,are available for purchasing one (or more) of four savings goals: home purchase; microenterprise capitalization; postsecondary education or training; and purchase of an automobile if necessary for employment or educational purposes.
	Technical Assistance	Discretionary—Cooperative agreement	Nonprofit organizations, voluntary agencies	Grants to enable organizations with expertise in a particular area to provide assistance to ORR-funded agencies.
	Microenterprise Development	Discretionary	Nonprofit organizations, voluntary agencies, state and local governments	Provides funding to assist refugees to become financiallyindependent by helping them develop capital resources and business expertise to start, expand, or strengthen their own businesses. Microenterprise projects typically include components of training and technical assistance in business skills and business management, credit assistance, and credit in the form of micro loans.
	Refugee Agricultural Partnership	Discretionary	Nonprofit organizations, voluntary agencies, state and local governments	Provides agricultural and food related resources and technical information to refugee families that are consistent with their agrarian backgrounds, and results inrural and urban farming projects that supports increased incomes, access to quality and familiar foods, better physical and mental health, and integration into this society.

Appendix IV: (Continued)

Agency	Grant	Type	Recipient	Description
	Supplemental Services for Recently Arrived Refugees	Discretionary	Nonprofit organizations, voluntary agencies, state and local governments	Provides funds to provide services to newly arriving refugees or sudden and unexpected large secondary migration of refugees where communities are not sufficiently prepared in terms of linguistic or culturally appropriate services and/or do not have sufficient service capacity.
	Ethnic Community Self-Help	Discretionary	Nonprofit organizations	Provides funds to support ethnic community based organizations in providing refugee populations with critical services to assist them in becoming integrated members of American society.

Sources: ORR annual report, ORR grant announcements, ORR program descriptions, the Catalog of Federal Domestic Assistance, and PRM grant announcements. ORR also funds additional programs for certain populations, including the Cuban Haitian Program, Anti-Trafficking in Persons Program, and an Unaccompanied Alien Children Program.

[a]For the purposes of this table, states refers to state agencies, state alternative programs, and state replacement designees. State alternative programs include (1) the Wilson/Fish program, which gives states flexibility in how they provide assistance to refugees, including whether to administer assistance primarily through local voluntary agencies, and (2) the Public Private Partnership program, which allows states to partner with local voluntary agencies to provide assistance. State replacement designees are authorized by ORR to administer assistance to refugees when a state withdraws from all or part of the refugee program.

[b]For the purposes of this table, refugees refers to refugees, certain Amerasians from Viet Nam, Cuban and Haitian entrants, asylees, victims of a severe form of trafficking, and Iraqi and Afghan Special Immigrants.

Appendix V: Status of Integration Working Group's Recommendations to ORR

In January 2007, ORR's Integration Working Group made short-term and long-term recommendations regarding ways in which ORR could more fully support the integration process for refugees.

	Implemented	**In process**	**Not implemented**
Short-term recommendations			
Include integration language in all grant announcements.	X		
Review discretionary grant programs offered in the standing announcement, ensuring that they promote integration.	X		
Establish the Department of Health and Human Services as the lead federal agency for integration.			X
Consider expanding ORR's discretionary programs.			X
Focus on integration in the areas of employment, English language acquisition, health, housing, and civic engagement.	X		
Focus technical assistance providers to support integration as an intentional process leading to civic engagement and citizenship.	X		
Seek and fund pilot programs such as the Building the New American Community project.			X
Develop an initiative to support professional recertification and credentialing for qualified individuals.		X	
Long-term recommendations			
Identify and share best practices through a survey of states, mutual aid associations, and voluntary agencies.	X		
Identify lessons learned, including case studies, from communities in which integration appears to be working well and where there are challenges.	X		

Appendix V: (Continued)

Study the effect of ORR policy and funding initiatives to promote integration over a three to five year period.			X
Refine/develop/disseminate an action model to be used for other immigrants and marginalized populations.			X
Seek broader collaboration with nonfederal entities such as private foundations, businesses, financial institutions, and the United Way.	X		

Sources: Report of the Integration Working Group, January 2007, and information provided by ORR.

End Notes

[1] According to data provided by the Department of State, 47 states and the District of Columbia resettled refugees in fiscal year 2011.

[2] See appendix II for a list of the studies we included in our literature review.

[3] We did not meet with all of these groups in every community we visited.

[4] As part of our site visit to Chicago, we also met with city officials in Skokie, Illinois. Our visit to the Detroit area focused on the cities of Dearborn and Sterling Heights, Michigan. Our visit to Seattle included interviews with relevant groups in Kent, Washington.

[5] 8 U.S.C. § 1101(a)(42)(A). In special circumstances, a refugee also may be a person who is within his or her country and who is persecuted or has a well-founded fear of persecution on account of race, religion, nationality, membership in a particular social group, or political opinion. Excluded from the definition of a refugee is any person who participated in the persecution of another.

[6] The Immigration and Nationality Act is Pub. L. No. 82-414, 66 Stat. 163 (1952) (codified as amended at 8 U.S.C. § 1101 et seq.). The Refugee Act of 1980 is Pub. L. No. 96-212, 94 Stat. 102. While the Immigration and Nationality Act, as amended, states that resettlement programs should help refugees achieve economic self-sufficiency as quickly as possible, it does not define economic self-sufficiency. HHS's Office of Refugee Resettlement defines economic self-sufficiency in its regulations as earning a total family income at a level that enables a family unit to support itself without receipt of a cash assistance grant. 45 C.F.R. § 400.2. Refugees may still be found economically self-sufficient if they receive other types of public noncash assistance, such as Supplemental Nutrition Assistance Program benefits or Medicaid.

[7] The Departments of State, Homeland Security, and Health and Human Services submit a report on behalf of the President to the Congress with their recommendation on how many refugees should be admitted, which according to Department of State officials, takes into account federal agencies' refugee processing capabilities.

[8] The number of refugees entering the United States has increased in recent years compared to the relatively low numbers entering after the terrorist attacks of September 11, 2001. In the aftermath of those attacks, a review of refugee-related security procedures was undertaken, refugee admissions were briefly suspended, and enhanced security measures were implemented. As a result of these and other factors, actual refugee admissions declined from 68,393 in fiscal year 2001 to 26,383 in fiscal year 2002 and 28,348 in fiscal year 2003. Admissions gradually increased and peaked at 74,652 in fiscal year 2009 and leveled off in 2010 with 73,311. Admissions decreased to a little over 56,000 in fiscal year 2011. According to the fiscal year 2012 refugee admissions proposal submitted to Congress by the Departments of State, Homeland Security, and Health and Human Services, this 2011 decrease was due largely to increased security clearance procedures.

[9] According to the Department of State, during weekly allocation meetings, cases with a tie in the United States are allocated to agencies with affiliates in communities where their friends or relatives live. National voluntary agencies then choose cases based on their total proposed capacity as well as local affiliates' capacity and resources. After the allocation meeting, the national voluntary agencies will assign individual cases to local affiliates based on a variety of factors, including ethnicity, language, family size, family composition, or medical conditions. For example, communities with an existing population of a particular ethnicity may have existing infrastructure for serving refugees of a particular ethnicity. Some communities are better able to accommodate larger families, while others may be more hospitable to single households.

[10] According to voluntary agency staff, they identify new communities to receive refugees based on requests from local stakeholders, recommendations by state officials, and the need to expand services to secondary migrants, refugees who migrate from their initial resettlement community to a community in another state.

[11] Participating organizations are expected to combine PRM's financial assistance with existing and projected private resources for the provision of reception and placement services.

[12] Not all refugees receive cash and medical assistance through ORR-funded programs. Refugees who are eligible for or who are receiving cash assistance from programs outside of ORR, such as Temporary Assistance for Needy Families or Supplemental Security Income, are generally not eligible to receive cash assistance from ORR's resettlement programs.

[13] GAO, *Refugee Assistance: Little is Known about Effectiveness of Different Approaches for Improving Refugees' Employment Outcomes,* GAO-11-369 (Washington, D.C.: Mar. 31, 2011). ORR also partially funds a separate Matching Grant program, administered by the national voluntary agencies. The Matching Grant program provides refugees with cash and other assistance for 4 to 6 months with the goal of helping them become self-sufficient without receiving cash benefits from a public assistance program. According to ORR, refugees who receive assistance from the Matching Grant program may not receive assistance or funding from any of ORR's other three assistance programs at the same time.

[14] The proposals typically include information on community capacity—such as employment rates, available healthcare, and housing—as well as information on the voluntary agency's organizational management plans and policies. PRM reviews and approves proposals from the national voluntary agencies.

[15] While some local affiliates may gather information about community-based factors by consulting with local stakeholders, others may choose to review publicly available information, such as the unemployment rate and rental prices.

[16] 8 U.S.C. § 1522(a)(1)(B)(iii).

[17] The cooperative agreements provide the conditions that the recipient must meet in exchange for receiving federal funding. The agreements signed by the national voluntary agencies also require them to ensure that their local affiliates participate in meetings called by state and local governments to coordinate plans for the placement of refugees. Similarly, ORR's regulations require states to provide an assurance in their state plan for refugee resettlement funds that local voluntary agencies and other community service agencies will meet with state and local governments at least quarterly to coordinate the appropriate placement of refugees in advance of the refugees' arrival. 45 C.F.R. § 400.5(h).

[18] For example, in fiscal year 2009, PRM required the voluntary agencies to provide the date and content of discussions with state and local stakeholders. In fiscal year 2010, PRM added a requirement for the voluntary agencies to include the results of those discussions. In 2012, PRM required voluntary agencies to include any concerns raised and compromises reached.

[19] General Dynamics Information Technology, Inc., *Building an Integrated Refugee Program*, a report prepared at the request of the Department of Health and Human Services Office of Refugee Resettlement (ORR), November 2009. Staff of Senate Committee on Foreign Relations, 111th Cong., Abandoned Upon Arrival: Implications for Refugees and Local Communities Burdened by a U.S. Resettlement System That is Not Working (Comm. Print 2010).

[20] According to PRM, in the past five years, affiliate abstracts submitted in annual proposals detail consultations and ongoing work with various state and local entities concerning placement in Clarkston. These consultations include regular meetings of the Georgia Coalition of Refugee Stakeholders, whose members include local elected officials. They also note discussions regarding housing, health services, and public school issues and consultations with the DeKalb county Board of Health/Refugee Clinic director and the DeKalb County school system. By request of the State Refugee Coordinator, in fiscal year 2011, refugee placements in Clarkston were reduced.

[21] These communities were recommended to us as examples of best practices.

[22] Data from the voluntary agency show that the number of newly arriving refugees in Fargo and West Fargo declined from 564 in fiscal year 2000 to 327 in fiscal year 2001 and to 42 in fiscal year 2002. Over the next 8 years, the number of new arrivals increased, but remained below the fiscal year 2000 level. In fiscal year 2010, there were 356 new arrivals.

[23] Codified at Tenn. Code Ann. §§ 4-38-101 to 4-38-104.

[24] The law also requires the state program office to provide a written quarterly report to local governments to plan and coordinate the placement of refugees, provide a quarterly report to specified state legislative committees, and ensure that host community residents and representatives of local governments are aware that they should notify the state program office with any concerns about resettlement activities.

[25] ORR officials noted, for example, that schools might receive additional federal funding if the proportion of low-income students in a school increases.

[26] According to ORR officials, the Department of Education provides supplemental funding under Title III of the Elementary and Secondary Education Act, as amended, Language Instruction for Limited English Proficient and Immigrant Students. However, school district officials in one community we visited said that continuous cuts in Title III funding have had significant impacts on schools that serve refugee students.

[27] ORR's regulations require that in providing refugee medical assistance, states must provide at least the same services in the same manner and to the same extent as under the state's Medicaid program. In addition, all recipients of federal funds are required to comply with Title VI of the Civil Rights Act of 1964, which prohibits discrimination based on race,

color, or national origin under any program receiving federal financial assistance. Several health care providers and voluntary agencies we spoke with viewed the hiring of interpreters as a way to comply with this requirement. This report, however, does not attempt to assess entities' compliance with Title VI requirements.

[28] Under Medicaid, states may claim federal matching funds for interpreter costs; however, in this case, the amount reimbursed by the state Medicaid program covered approximately half of the cost of the interpreter services, which left the provider to cover the remaining cost.

[29] For fiscal year 2012, the school impact grant program provided funding to states ranging from $150,000 to $1 million, depending on the size of the school-age refugee population and other eligible populations. States used these funds to award grants to state departments of education, local school districts, or voluntary agencies.

[30] Under the Elementary and Secondary Education Act, as amended, all students are expected to meet or exceed state standards in reading and in math by 2014. Each state establishes its own definition of adequate yearly progress to determine school and school district achievement toward this goal.

[31] According to PRM officials, refugees often migrate multiple times. Officials also noted that some refugees who choose to migrate from their initial resettlement communities do so within a few months of arrival, while others do so after a longer period of time.

[32] According to PRM data for fiscal year 2011, 3,261 refugees, or 5.7 percent of refugees, moved away from their initial resettlement community within the first 90 days of resettlement. According to ORR data for fiscal year 2010, states reported that approximately 11,143 refugees moved from their initial resettlement state. ORR collects secondary migration data on refugees who have arrived within 36 months prior to the beginning of the fiscal year. Fiscal year 2010 data showed that Texas and California had large numbers of refugees moving both in and out. There was strong net migration into Minnesota, Florida, Colorado, Ohio, and Kansas. There was strong net migration out of Arizona, New York, New Jersey, Texas, and Georgia.

[33] Depending on the program in which they are enrolled, refugees are eligible to receive ORR-funded cash assistance for 8 months if they are enrolled in a statewide program. Refugees enrolled in a Matching Grant program are eligible to receive cash assistance for 4 to 6 months after arrival. Refugees are also eligible for ORR-funded medical assistance for up to 8 months after arrival. Refugees are eligible to receive services through ORR's social services grant program for up to 5 years after arrival.

[34] Refugee social services programs provide employment and other services such as social adjustment, translation, childcare, and citizenship services, as well as case management. ORR allocates these funds to states based on estimates of arriving refugees, as well as secondary migration data for the prior 2 years. These social services funds do not increase within a given year if the number of refugees served is greater than anticipated.

[35] General Dynamics Information Technology, Inc., *Building an Integrated Refugee Program.*

[36] According to ORR officials, less than 10 percent of the data submitted on secondary migrants are rejected.

[37] To be considered for the Supplemental Services for Recently Arrived Refugees grant, communities must demonstrate situations such as (1) refugee services do not presently exist or the service capacity is not sufficient to accommodate significant increases in arrivals; and/or (2) the existing service system does not have culturally and linguistically appropriate services. ORR provides grantees with funding for a grant project period of17 months.

[38] Spring Institute for Intercultural Learning. *Rural Secondary Migration Pilot Project: Impacts, Challenges, and Opportunities,*, a report prepared at the request of the Department of Health and Human Services Office of Refugee Resettlement (ORR), October 2009.

[39] General Dynamics Information Technology, Inc., *Building an Integrated Refugee Program.*

[40] PRM initially limited resettlement in these cities to immediate family members of refugees who were already living there. However, in response to requests from the local voluntary agencies and a leveling in the flow of arrivals, the metro Detroit policy was amended to allow placement of any refugees with ties to family or friends in the area. According to voluntary agency officials, the policy was amended due to high levels of secondary migration and the difficulty serving secondary migrants without funding.

[41] PRM has discretion to approve or deny this request, as state law is not binding on the federal government.

[42] 8 U.S.C. § 1522(a)(1)(A)(i). This law requires ORR to do so to the extent of available appropriations.

[43] Cash assistance includes both refugee cash assistance and payments received under the Temporary Assistance for Needy Families program.

[44] Employment is measured for all cash assistance recipients, but after cash assistance expires, employment is measured only for refugees who are enrolled in ORR-funded employment assistance. The portion of the caseload that is receiving employment services but not receiving cash assistance varies widely by state. For example, in 2010 in California, 12 percent of the caseload was not receiving federal cash assistance, but in Wisconsin, 66 percent of the caseload was receiving no federal cash assistance. ORR requires service providers to give newly arrived refugees priority for services. Some service providers have said that in order to ensure that new arrivals continued to receive needed services, they provided employment services to refugees for only about 1 year rather than the 5 years allowed.

[45] Our 2011 report provides more information about the various ways states may opt to deliver services. See GAO-11-369. All states, except Wyoming, administer an ORRfunded assistance program that provides up to 8 months of cash and medical assistance, as well as other social services. In addition, some refugees participate in the Matching Grant program, which is only partially funded by ORR. According to ORR, a network of national voluntary agencies administers this program. The Matching Grant program provides refugees with cash and other assistance for 4 to 6 months with the goal of helping them become self-sufficient without receiving cash benefits from a public assistance program.

[46] States do report to ORR the number of refugees they serve who have been in the United States for more than 12 months. ORR officials noted that refugees may also access mainstream employment services.

[47] Obtaining credentials may require additional training, including English language training, which may go beyond 6 or 8 months.

[48] A study commissioned by ORR on its social service and targeted assistance grant highlighted a career-laddering program in Miami as a promising practice. The purpose of the program is to help refugees who were professionals in their native countries but who lack certification to do similar work in the United States. The program helps refugees with obtaining credentials, training, and employment in a field that is consistent with their career goals and similar to the work they did in their native countries. HHS, *The Evaluation of the Refugee Social Service (RSS) and Targeted Assistance Formula Grant (TAG) Programs: Synthesis of Findings from Three Sites* (Washington, D.C.: March 2008). ORR also partially funds two other programs that promote professional recertification of refugee physicians and other

highly skilled professionals. One is located in Minnesota. The other is located in San Diego, California.

[49] The individual development account program provides refugees with matched savings accounts for the purchase of specific assets: a home, capital for a small business, post-secondary education or training, and in some cases, the purchase of a car if needed to maintain or upgrade employment.

[50] This definition is the working definition adopted by ORR's integration working group, and is not an official definition adopted by ORR. ORR created an integration working group in 2006 to review and analyze the integration process for refugees in communities throughout the United States.

[51] PRM offers cultural orientation in both overseas locations and the resettlement location in the United States, and recently piloted English language training programs in Kenya, Thailand, and Nepal.

[52] ORR's mission statement is: "Founded on the belief that newly arriving populations have inherent capabilities when given opportunities, the Office of Refugee Resettlement (ORR) provides people in need with critical resources to assist them in becoming integrated members of American society." ORR's major goal is to "provide assistance to refugees and other eligible persons through its various programs and grants, so that they can achieve self-sufficiency and integration within the shortest time period after arriving in the United States."

[53] The micro-enterprise assistance program provides refugees with loans and training to start, expand, or strengthen their own businesses. As noted above, the individual development account program provides refugees with matched savings accounts for the purchase of specific assets, including capital for a small business.

[54] See appendix V for a complete list of the working group's recommendations to ORR and their implementation status.

[55] ISED Solutions, *Exploring Refugee Integration: Experiences in Four American Communities*, a report prepared at the request of the Department of Health and Human Services Office of Refugee Resettlement (ORR), June 2010. We included this study in our literature review.

[56] Each year, an ORR contractor surveys a random sample of refugees selected from the population of all refugees who arrived in the U.S. in the last 5 years.

[57] For example, the survey response rate was 50.3 percent in 2008 and 36.6 percent in 2007.

[58] See appendix II for a list of the studies we included in our literature review.

End Notes for Appendix I

[1] We did not meet with all of these groups in every community we visited.

[2] As part of our site visit to Chicago, we also met with city officials in Skokie, Illinois. Our visit to the Detroit area focused on the cities of Dearborn and Sterling Heights, Michigan. Our visit to Seattle included interviews with relevant groups in Kent, Washington.

[3] We excluded studies addressing refugees' integration into the countries where they first sought asylum.

[4] See appendix II for a list of the studies we included in our literature review.

INDEX

A

B

C

D

E

F

G

H

M

N

O

P

R

S

T